AMERICA
THE VEGETARIAN TABLE

BY DEBORAH MADISON

PHOTOGRAPHY BY DEBORAH JONES

FOOD STYLING BY SANDRA COOK

CHRONICLE BOOKS · SAN FRANCISCO

DEDICATION

To my father, John H. Madison, whose long-abiding passion for growing the good food
gave me my love for quince, Concord grape pie, heirloom apples, Jersey cows—
in short, the gift of my own American culinary roots.

Library of Congress Cataloging-in-Publication Data:
Madison, Deborah.
The vegetarian table. America/Deborah Madison.
p. cm.
Includes index.
ISBN 0-8118-0888-2 (hc)
1. Vegetarian cookery. 2. Cookery, American. I. Title.
TX837.M2362 1996
641.5' 636' 0973—dc20 95-50303
CIP

Book Design: Louise Fili Ltd.
Design Assistant: Tonya Hudson
Photo Styling: Sara Slavin

Printed in Hong Kong.

Distributed in Canada by Raincoast Books,
8680 Cambie St., Vancouver, B.C. V6P 6M9

10 9 8 7 6 5 4 3 2 1

Chronicle Books
275 Fifth Street
San Francisco, CA 94103

CONTENTS

ACKNOWLEDGMENTS

I AM GRATEFUL TO BILL LEBLOND, OF CHRONICLE BOOKS, FOR SUGGESTING THAT I WRITE **THE VEGETARIAN TABLE: AMERICA**, AND TO MY AGENT, DOE COOVER, FOR SAYING DO IT! Without them, I might never have thought about American food and its history, a subject I will now pursue. For the opportunity to spend many hours studying community cookbooks, I am grateful to the Schlesinger Library, particularly to Barbara Haber, curator of books, and Barbara Wheaton, honorary curator of the culinary collection, for enthusiastically pointing me in interesting directions. Heartfelt thanks are given to Kathi Long, for her cooking companionship and valued second opinions in the kitchen, to Marion Cunningham for her ready willingness to entertain my questions about American cooking, and to Linda Funk of the Wisconsin Milk Marketing Board for introducing me to some excellent new American cheeses. Without kind persistence from my editor, Leslie Jonath, this book would undoubtedly be lingering in the research stage. And lastly, my admiration for those early Americans who, trudging long distances into the unknown with little more than courage, hope, and a handful of seeds, laid down our culinary roots.

DEBORAH JONES WISHES TO THANK SARA SLAVIN, FOR HER PROP STYLING; JERI JONES, FOR ASSISTING WITH THE PHOTOGRAPHY; ALLYSON LEVY, FOR ASSISTING WITH THE FOOD STYLING; AND DONALD SHECKLER, FOR THE SPECIAL PROPS HE PROVIDED.

INTRODUCTION

❈

I CONFESS THAT I BEGAN **THE VEGETARIAN TABLE: AMERICA** WITH SOME DISMAY. WE DON'T THINK OF AMERICAN FOOD AS BEING RICH WITH VEGETABLE DISHES THE WAY, FOR INSTANCE, THE CUISINES OF THE MEDITERRANEAN COUNTRIES ARE. For one thing, outside of California, we don't have the kind of climate that supports a heavily plant-based cuisine. Nor do we have the historical inclination to eat that way. Vegetables have always rested on the periphery of our plate. But after looking at our food habits and history through community cookbooks, I gained a new appreciation of who we have been at the table, and where it is we might be going. The story of American food is filled with struggle but also with gems of information and sensibilities that are close to our own today, as well as some that are as different as day from night.

Starting out in a new and utterly foreign land is clearly a difficult challenge. In addition to the obvious physical and emotional hardships, America's early settlers didn't arrive with much of their familiar food. Nor did they arrive knowing the conditions of the soil, or the beginnings and endings of the seasons where they settled, and other vital facts that would help to ensure them some success replicating the gardens left behind. From the beginning, completely new, unfamiliar foods—corn, Jerusalem artichokes, beans, squashes and pumpkins, seeds and berries—generously shared by those already living here, would of necessity become significant, then remain over time as a part of the national table.

During the early years, the colonists ate very lean. Their main sources of fat were egg yolks and the little fat found in game. Once livestock arrived in 1611, animal husbandry flourished, and by 1650 there was a wealth of domesticated animals. For a mobile people with much land to settle, live animals were easier to move from place to place than vegetable gardens and orchards, whose cultivation requires time and history. This practical consideration alone would help make meat the more prevalent food. Add to this the fact that early vegetable gardening, without special seeds for particular climates, greenhouses, or other gardening aids, demanded that the seasons be absolutely respected. Given that California wouldn't be put to large-scale farming for quite some time, and that the means to extend an ample harvest through commercial canning, refrigeration, freezing, and shipping were far in the distance, it is not surprising that we didn't develop the kind of plant-based repertoire that Mediterranean countries enjoy. Put simply, plant foods have been hard won.

My doubts about finding usable old recipes were partially well founded. A lot of vegetables are covered with thick white sauces and cracker crusts. Sometimes potatoes are deep-fried and then baked. Or tomato pies are slathered with mayonnaise, vegetables are stewed in vinegar and sugar, and sugar appears where it has no need to be. While today these treatments seem excessive, they may have existed in order to provide a way for everyone at the early American table to have a bite of something that was fairly scarce. The additions of sugar, salt, vinegar, and fat made vegetables go further, for highly acid, sweet, or salty foods can't be eaten in large amounts, and fat is itself filling, triggering feelings of satisfaction. Other food habits originated from bygone necessities. Whereas women once canned or "put-up" a harvest of fruits and vegetables, our modern reliance on canned goods is mostly habit, since fresh produce is now available year-round.

In the past, the food supply had its own rhythm of waxings and wanings, a rhythm that was reflected in some of our recipes and ways of doing things. For example, some dishes are shocking by today's standards for the numbers of eggs they contain—fifteen eggs in a moussaka! But people worked hard, eggs were appreciated for their protein, and there are times when chickens naturally lay more heavily. The other side of such largess was that when the chickens weren't laying—and they weren't always forced to lay all year the way they are today—the few precious eggs there were reserved for the sick.

There are also wonderfully appealing recipes guided by common sense, thrift, and the blessing of limitations. The restraint of seasoning, a characteristic of traditional American food that many of us have tried to overcome by having a wild hand with herbs, spices, chiles, and vinegars, in fact results in food that tastes pure and readable. The cloves and lemon in a Boston black bean soup are a revelation, not because of mysterious layerings of flavors, but because they let us know exactly where we are. The directness of flavor in American food calms the palate, then exhilarates it with its clarity. Some might call it plain, but it is at times sure, straightforward, and elegant.

The key to food that is both simple and sublime has always been good ingredients. Twenty years after the American revolution, Amelia Simmons, in her book *American Cookery*, wrote that "the best cook cannot alter the first quality. They [the vegetables] must be good or the cook will be disappointed." In other words, we can't end up with something better than what we start with. In 1900, a senator's wife, moved to Washington from Iowa, corroborated this, writing rather listlessly, "Of late, with only the fruit to be found in the Washington market, not always so fresh nor 'just ripe enough'—I undertake but a few things, jellies and jams mostly." Why jams and jellies? Because sugar replaces the lack of flavor with sweetness (a taste sensation we Americans today know better than we know flavor). The importance of quality is a truth that seems to need repeating. Amelia Simmons's remark was echoed two hundred years later in a California garden by the English biodynamic gardener Alan Chadwick, when he pronounced, "Cooking begins in the garden; we only finish it in the kitchen." Cooks know this to be true, which is why the garden and the farmers' market have become such important resources for anyone who wants to cook easily and cook well.

Today's campaign to encourage Americans to eat more fruits and vegetables isn't new. You can almost hear the urgency in the voice of a contributor to the *Economy Administration Cookbook* (1913): "Nutrition experts are today crying from the housetops the importance and economy of serving generously fresh fruits and vegetables in their seasons." And now, the new dietary guidelines give a prominent place to fruits and vegetables. It has been hard for us to have a national love affair with vegetables, but perhaps it is finally beginning to happen. There is a passion for vegetables now, and we're finding that we can take vegetables from their satellite position on the plate and shift them to the center.

American cooking has been formed by all who have settled here, as well as geography and climate. It is still being shaped today by our immigrant citizens, our exposure to the rest of the world through travel, and the enormous availability of new foods. In a book this small it is simply not possible to include everyone and the contributions they've made. I chose to start with our history rather than our present, and along the way I fell in love with many recipes. Taken together, the recipes I've chosen provide a sort of through-line that carries us into the present, with the use of modern ingredients and sensibilities. Even though they are informed by, if not firmly rooted in, our various pasts, these are American recipes that have life in them and the capacity to bring nourishment and pleasure to the table.

chapter one

PICKLES AND PRESERVES

PICKLES AND PRESERVES

GIVEN LONG WINTERS, UNFAMILIAR GROWING CONDITIONS, AND THE GENERAL DIFFICULTIES OF SETTLING IN A NEW LAND, THE PRESERVATION OF FOOD WAS OF GREAT IMPORTANCE TO EARLY AMERICANS. Making pickles and preserves was one way of keeping the harvest. Since much of early preserving relied on using a great deal of vinegar, sugar, and salt—in contrast to drying, canning, or freezing—condiments were the result.

Collectively known as sweets and sours, the well-provided Pennsylvania Dutch meal boasted seven of each on the table. Many are still familiar to us today, such as sweet-and-spicy melon rinds and pickled beets. But the earlier colonists pickled more than familiar garden vegetables. In *Martha Washington's Book of Cookery* there are references to recipes for pickled kidney beans, lettuce stalks, purslane, the buds of the Scotch broom, medicinal flowers, wood sorrel, and other wild foods that point to the necessity of thrift and the making use of what the land provided on its own, as well as its more tended offerings.

There are still those who put up cucumbers and peaches by the bushel, but most of us don't. Nowadays, it seems that storage space is often at too great a premium. Still, a pint of homemade pickles is a nice thing to bring to the table, and they needn't be made to last the winter. These modern versions of old recipes are well reduced in size and made to be stored in the refrigerator and enjoyed over a period of weeks and months, rather than seasons. Of course, they can be properly canned, if you wish to do so. In any case, they make a refreshing counterpoint to the flavors and textures of most foods we eat and are particularly pretty garnishes to include with a sandwich.

PICTURED, CLOCKWISE FROM TOP: PICKLED BEETS (PAGE 14),
SPICED CANTALOUPE PICKLES (PAGE 16), AND SPICED QUINCE (PAGE 17).

PICKLED BEETS

MAKES ABOUT 1 QUART

PRETTIEST ARE TINY GARDEN BEETS, ABOUT AS BIG AS LARGE MARBLES, PICKLED WHOLE. OTHER-WISE, USE FULL-SIZED BEETS, PEELED AND CUT INTO QUARTERS, BEFORE STEAMING. ONCE PICK-LED, THE BEETS CAN BE SLICED THINLY OR SERVED IN LARGE PIECES.

20 small beets (about 3 cups)

1½ cups apple cider vinegar

1 cup water

½ cup white or light brown sugar

1 teaspoon salt

1 scant teaspoon freshly grated nutmeg

1 ounce fresh ginger, peeled and sliced
    into strips

2 tablespoons coarsely grated fresh
    horseradish

7 whole cloves

Trim the beets, leaving on ½ inch of their stems, and scrub them well. Steam them until tender but still a little firm, about 15 minutes. Let the beets cool. If the skins are tender looking and free of roots or coarse patches, leave them unpeeled; otherwise, peel them. Fit them into a clean quart jar.

Combine the remaining ingredients in a nonreactive saucepan and bring them to a boil, stirring to dissolve the sugar. Pour the hot vinegar mixture over the beets, immersing them fully. Cover tightly and store in the refrigerator. They are best served after sitting for at least a day and will keep for one to two months.

PICKLED CUCUMBERS AND ONIONS WITH FRESH DILL

I THINK OF THIS AS AN AUGUST GARDEN OR MARKET PICKLE, ALTHOUGH IT IS SOMETIMES CALLED A LAZY PICKLE BECAUSE IT'S SO QUICK TO MAKE. IT NEEDS 3 HOURS TO CURE AND WILL STAY FRESH FOR ABOUT A WEEK. A DISTILLED WHITE VINEGAR WOULD BE APPROPRIATE HERE, BUT JAPANESE RICE WINE VINEGAR, WITH ITS LOW ACIDITY AND SWEET TASTE, IS ALSO A GOOD CHOICE—IF NOT A MORE INTERESTING ONE.

Peel the cucumbers, halve them lengthwise, and neatly scoop out the seeds with a spoon. Slice them thinly crosswise. Quarter the onion and slice thinly crosswise as well.

Put the salt, pepper, and sugar in a bowl large enough to hold the vegetables. Add the vinegar and water and stir to dissolve the sugar and salt. Then add the cucumbers, onion, and dill and push down on them to submerge them. Cover and refrigerate at least 3 hours before serving. To serve, drain off the juice, but reserve it to use for covering any pickles that are left.

2 small, firm cucumbers, about ¾ pound total

1 small red onion, fresh from the garden if possible

½ teaspoon salt

freshly ground white pepper

1 tablespoon sugar

1 cup distilled white vinegar or rice wine vinegar

1 cup water

2 tablespoons chopped dill

SPICED CANTALOUPE PICKLES

MAKES ABOUT 1 QUART

DON'T USE A DEAD-RIPE MELON FOR THIS SWEET PICKLE, AS IT WILL BE TOO SOFT. SELECT ONE THAT'S STILL SLIGHTLY FIRM YET RIPE AND FILLED WITH FLAVOR.

1 cantaloupe, about 2 pounds

1½ cups apple cider vinegar

½ cup water

1½ teaspoons salt

1½ cups sugar

4 cinnamon sticks, each about
    3 inches long

1 teaspoon whole cloves

Cut the cantaloupe in half, remove and discard the seeds, and cut into wedges no more than 1½ inches thick at the center. Slice the melon off its rind and cut it into 1-inch chunks. Put it in a bowl with the vinegar and water and let stand at room temperature overnight.

The next day, transfer the melon and liquid to a nonreactive saucepan, add the remaining ingredients, and bring to a boil. Lower the heat and cook, uncovered, at a slow boil until the melon looks translucent, about 1 hour and 10 minutes. Ladle into a clean quart jar, cover tightly, and store in the refrigerator. They are best served after sitting for at least a day and will keep for one to two months.

SPICED QUINCE

MAKES ABOUT 1 QUART

QUINCE TREES, WHICH WERE POPULAR WITH OUR ENGLISH FOREBEARERS, CAME EARLY TO AMERICA. IN THE FALL YOU CAN SOMETIMES FIND OLD TREES COVERED WITH THEIR LUMINOUS GOLDEN FRUITS. THE SPICES CALLED FOR HERE ARE MORE COMMONLY USED WITH PEACHES AND PEARS, BUT I ESPECIALLY LIKE THEM WITH QUINCES. IF COOKED LONG ENOUGH, THE FRUITS TURN A DUSKY PINK BUT DON'T LOSE THEIR TEXTURE. THEY'LL KEEP FOR THE WINTER IN THE REFRIGERATOR, WHERE THEY CAN BE DRAWN OUT AS NEEDED. INSTEAD OF THE USUAL CRANBERRIES AT HOLIDAY MEALS, SIMMER A BAG OF THEM WITH THE COOKED QUINCES. IT'S A GORGEOUS-LOOKING DISH, A LITTLE UNEXPECTED, AND WONDERFUL SERVED CHILLED.

Cut each quince into eighths, carefully peel them, and then cut out the cores. Put the trimmings and cores in a saucepan with the water, bring to a boil, and then simmer for 25 minutes to make a quince-flavored "stock." Strain into a nonreactive saucepan and add the remaining ingredients, including the quince. Bring to a boil, stirring to dissolve the sugar. Lower the heat and simmer, covered, until the quinces are deep pink, about 3 hours. Keep an eye on the liquid to make sure there's enough. Add more water if the fruits begin to dry out.

Taste and if you care for a little more tartness, add the balsamic vinegar. A teaspoon or two should do it. Ladle into a clean quart jar, cover tightly, and store in the refrigerator. They are best served after sitting for at least a day and will keep for up to three months.

2 pounds ripe, golden quinces

4 cups water

1 cup apple cider vinegar

2 cups sugar

1 teaspoon whole cloves

1 cinnamon stick, about 3 inches long

5 slices fresh ginger

balsamic vinegar to taste

PEAR CHUTNEY

MAKES ABOUT 2½ CUPS

CHUTNEYS ARE SWEETS AND SOURS IN A SINGLE JAR. FIRM BUT RIPE FRUITS ARE THE BEST TO USE — LITTLE WINTER NELLIS, ANJOU, OR BARTLETT PEARS THAT ARE A DAY SHY OF EATING. PEACHES AND NECTARINES CAN ALSO BE USED FOR THIS CHUTNEY.

2 pounds firm pears
½ cup white sugar
1 cup apple cider vinegar
1 cup light brown sugar
½ cup golden raisins
finely chopped zest of 1 lemon
1½ teaspoons ground coriander
1 teaspoon minced garlic
¼ cup peeled and diced or sliced
   fresh ginger
¾ cup finely chopped white onion
3 dried cayenne, árbol, or other slender
   dried hot chiles
10 whole cloves

Peel and core the pears and dice them into small pieces. Put them in a heavy saucepan with the white sugar and place over low heat. Cook until they've released quite a bit of juice, 5 to 10 minutes. Stir them a few times while they cook. Drain off the juice and set the pears and juice aside separately.

In a nonreactive pot, combine the remaining ingredients and bring to a boil. Add the reserved juice, lower the heat, and simmer until fine bubbles dot the surface, about 40 minutes. Add the reserved pears and cook over low heat until the pears are translucent and the sauce is quite reduced and thick, about 25 minutes more. Ladle into a clean jar, cover tightly, and refrigerate. They are best served after sitting for at least a day and will keep for up to two months.

APPLESAUCE

SERVES 4 TO 6

S IMPLE, PRACTICAL, AND VERSATILE, APPLESAUCE IS A BREAKFAST FRUIT, A LIGHT DESSERT, OR A SWEET-TART ACCOMPANIMENT TO A MAIN DISH, SUCH AS THE WALNUT AND POTATO CROQUETTES ON PAGE 97. WHEN MADE WITH THE FIRST APPLES OF THE SEASON, IT'S ASTONISHINGLY VIBRANT, BUT IT'S ALSO THE PERFECT PLACE TO USE WINDFALLS OR APPLES THAT ARE NO LONGER GOOD ENOUGH TO SERVE OUTRIGHT. MIX VARIETIES OR SELECT FOR A TARTER OR SWEETER END RESULT. IF THEY HAVEN'T BEEN WAXED, COOK THE APPLES WITH THE SKINS ON, AND ALWAYS INCLUDE SOME RED ONES — YOU'LL END UP WITH A ROSY PINK SAUCE. A FOOD MILL SAVES PEELING AND CORING.

Cut each apple into sixths. Don't bother to remove the cores and skins. Put them in a heavy saucepan, add the water, cover tightly, and cook over medium heat until the apples are completely soft, about 25 minutes. They should yield plenty of their own juices, but check the pan once or twice just to make sure.

Pass them through a food mill to rid them of their skins and seeds and return them to the pot. Add sugar or honey to taste—late-harvest apples may need hardly any—and cook over medium heat, stirring occasionally, until it has dissolved. Add lemon juice if the apples need a tarter edge, and season with the cinnamon or cardamom and nutmeg to taste. If the sauce is very thin, continue cooking it over low heat to cook off the extra moisture. Transfer to a clean jar or covered container and refrigerate. It should keep for 2 to 3 weeks.

You can also make applesauce in a pressure cooker. Add the cut apples and a few tablespoons of water, bring pressure to high for 10 minutes, then let it return to zero slowly. The apples will be soft, ready to pass through the food mill.

8 to 10 apples
½ cup water
sugar or honey
fresh lemon juice, if apples are sweet
1 teaspoon ground cinnamon or
*   cardamom, or to taste*
few gratings of nutmeg

SALSA

MAKES ABOUT 1 CUP

A S NEARLY EVERYONE KNOWS, SALSA HAS OVERTAKEN KETCHUP AS A CONDIMENT ON THE AMERI-CAN TABLE AND THE NUMBER AND VARIETY OF BOTTLED SALSAS — AND THEIR RELATIVES, SAM-BALS AND CHUTNEYS — ON THE MARKET ARE SEEMINGLY WITHOUT END. HERE'S THE MOST BASIC ONE, KNOWN AS **PICO DE GALLO, SALSA CRUDA,** OR **SALSA MEXICANA.** IT'S THE ONE YOU FIND ON THE TABLE IN EVERY MEXICAN RESTAURANT, THE ONE FOR DIPPING CHIPS OR SPOONING OVER A QUESADILLA OR TACO. BEGIN WITH GOOD-TASTING, RIPE TOMATOES AND PLAN TO USE THE SAUCE WITHIN THE DAY.

3 ripe tomatoes

2 or 3 serrano chiles

10 cilantro sprigs, chopped

¼ cup finely diced white or red onion

½ teaspoon salt

1 teaspoon fresh lime juice, or to taste

a few tablespoons water

Cut the tomatoes in half around the equator and pull out the seeds with your fingers. Chop them into small pieces and put them in a bowl. Finely dice the chiles as well, leaving the seeds in for more heat, or taking them out if you want less. Add them to the tomatoes along with the cilantro, onion, and salt. Stir in the lime juice. If the sauce doesn't seem juicy enough, stir in the water.

TOMATO KETCHUP

KETCHUP GOES BACK A LONG WAY IN OUR CULINARY HISTORY, AND THE VERSIONS POPULAR IN THE EARLY NINETEENTH CENTURY WERE GENEROUSLY SPICED AND SCARCELY SWEETENED, A FAR CRY FROM TODAY'S SUGARY PRODUCTS. YOU'LL NEED A GLUT OF RIPE, RED TOMATOES. APPLE CIDER VINEGAR WOULD BE TRADITIONAL, BUT I THINK THE DENSE, SWEET FLAVOR OF GOOD BALSAMIC WORKS WELL, TOO. YOU MIGHT WANT TO ADD A TOUCH OF APPLE CIDER VINEGAR AT THE END TO BRING UP THE ACID. ❀ IF YOU USE A FOOD MILL, YOU DON'T HAVE TO PEEL THE TOMATOES, SINCE IT SEPARATES OUT THE SKINS AND SEEDS. IF NOT, PEEL, HALVE, AND SEED THE TOMATOES BEFORE DICING, AND THEN PURÉE IN A BLENDER.

Cut the tomatoes into chunks. Put them into a heavy pot (but not a nonreactive one) with the onion and stew, uncovered, over medium heat until they are well broken down, about 40 minutes. Pass through a food mill placed over a bowl, or purée in a blender if already peeled and seeded.

Return the purée to the pot and add the cinnamon, celery seeds, mace, cloves, allspice, and cayenne. Place over medium-low heat and simmer until thick, stirring frequently. When it's ketchup-thick, after 40 minutes to 1 hour, add the salt, sugar or honey, and the balsamic vinegar. Acidity in tomatoes varies, so taste and adjust with salt, sugar, and the balsamic and cider vinegars until you get the balance the way you like it. Pour into a clean quart jar, cover tightly, and store in the refrigerator. The ketchup should keep several months.

5 pounds ripe, meaty tomatoes such as beefsteaks

1 large yellow or red onion, diced

1 teaspoon ground cinnamon

½ teaspoon celery seeds

½ teaspoon ground mace

½ teaspoon ground cloves

½ teaspoon ground allspice

⅛ teaspoon cayenne pepper

½ teaspoon salt

1 tablespoon brown sugar or honey, or to taste

¼ cup balsamic vinegar

apple cider vinegar to taste

CRANBERRY RELISH

MAKES ABOUT 2½ CUPS

TODAY, DRIED CRANBERRIES HAVE BECOME POPULAR, BUT WE'LL PROBABLY ALWAYS PERSIST IN INCLUDING FRESH CRANBERRIES AT OUR THANKSGIVING MEAL—EITHER JELLIED, COOKED, OR MADE INTO THIS SWEET-TART RELISH. OFTEN COOKS HAPPILY REMARK THAT YOU CAN MAKE THIS WITH THE WHOLE ORANGE, PEEL AND ALL, BUT SOME PEOPLE PREFER TO TAKE THE TIME TO CUT AWAY THE WHITE SKIN JUST UNDER THE PEEL, WHERE THE FRUIT'S BITTERNESS LIES. WHILE THERE'S NO URGENT NEED TO CHANGE THE ORIGINAL RECIPE, I FIND SOME TANGERINE PEEL AND A PINCH OF CLOVE SPICE THINGS UP A BIT, YET THE FEEL OF THE FAMILIAR DISH IS RETAINED. CRANBERRY RELISH CAN BE MADE SEVERAL DAYS AHEAD OF TIME, WHICH ALLOWS THE FLAVORS TO RIPEN.

Sort through the cranberries, since there are always some soft, squishy ones. Discard them and rinse the rest. Score the orange into 4 sections, remove the peel, then slice off the thin white membrane with a knife. Halve the tangerines across their equators and remove the seeds.

Put the orange peels and tangerines in a food processor and coarsely chop them into small pieces, about as big as a dime. Add the cranberries and nuts and pulse just enough to make a coarse relish. It shouldn't be a purée. Remove to a clean bowl and stir in the sugar and cloves. Cover and refrigerate overnight or longer before serving.

4 cups cranberries (about 1 pound)

1 navel orange

2 tangerines

1½ cups sugar

⅛ teaspoon ground cloves

½ to 1 cup walnuts or pecans

MARINATED BABY ARTICHOKES

MAKES 2 PINTS

THOSE WHO LOVE MARINATED ARTICHOKES IN A SALAD OR ON AN ANTIPASTO PLATE WILL BE MAD ABOUT THESE PLUMP WHOLE ARTICHOKES PACKED IN OLIVE OIL WITH BRANCHES OF HERBS. ✸ THE "BABIES" ARE THE ARTICHOKES THAT FORM AT THE BASE OF THE PLANT. SHELTERED FROM THE LIGHT AND HEAT OF THE SUN, THEY DON'T GROW TO FULL SIZE. IN CONTRAST, THOSE THAT FORM ON THE TOP OF THE SAME PLANT CAN WEIGH CLOSE TO A POUND EACH. PAUL BERTOLLI'S RECIPE IN **CHEZ PANISSE COOKING** INSPIRED THIS ONE. I'VE MADE MY OWN VARIATIONS USING DRIED OREGANO INSTEAD OF THYME, OR QUARTERING THE ARTICHOKES RATHER THAN LEAVING THEM WHOLE.

juice of 2 lemons

4 pounds baby artichokes

3 cups white wine vinegar or
tarragon vinegar

2 cups water

4 small bay leaves

4 whole cloves

½ teaspoon peppercorns

4 small dried red chiles

12 thyme or tarragon sprigs

2 teaspoons salt

extra-virgin olive oil as needed
(2 to 3 cups)

10 cloves garlic

Have ready a large bowl to which you have added the lemon juice. Snap off the outer 3 or 4 layers of leaves from the artichokes until you reach the pale inner leaves. Slice off the top half of the leaves, removing all the prickly leaf points, and trim the stems and base. As you work, put the artichokes into the bowl, adding water to cover.

In a medium stainless-steel saucepan, combine the vinegar, water, bay leaves, cloves, peppercorns, one of the chiles, and 4 of the thyme or tarragon sprigs. Bring to a boil, add the salt, and then add the artichokes. Reduce the heat and simmer until firm but tender, about 10 minutes. Drain, reserving the seasonings.

Meanwhile, sterilize 2 pint jars, lids, and ring bands in boiling water and drain well on a clean kitchen towel. Pack the artichokes into the hot jars along with the drained seasonings, the remaining thyme or tarragon sprigs and chiles, and the garlic cloves. Arrange the artichokes so that their cut tops are facing the glass, and position the herb sprigs so that they are visible. When the jars are nearly full, pour in enough olive oil to immerse the artichokes completely. Cover with the lids and screw on the ring bands. Immerse the jars in boiling water for 10 minutes. Store in a cool, dark place. Let sit at least 1 week before using. Once opened, store in the refrigerator. The oil, which will be deliciously flavored with the herbs and garlic, can be used for cooking, on pasta, or in vinaigrettes.

PEPPER SAUCE AND PICKLED PEPPERS

MAKES ALMOST 2 CUPS

PEPPER SAUCE—VINEGAR MADE HOT BY PICKLING HOT PEPPERS—IS AN ESSENTIAL SOUTHERN CONDIMENT. THE BITE OF THE PEPPERS AND THE ACID NIP OF THE VINEGAR ALWAYS ADD GREATLY TO GREENS, BOTH TEMPERING AND SHARPENING THEIR TASTE, BE THEY MUSTARD, COLLARDS, SPINACH, OR ANOTHER VEGETABLE ALTOGETHER, SUCH AS BROCCOLI. THE PEPPERS CAN BE RETRIEVED AND SERVED AS WELL, MAKING A RATHER FEISTY PICKLE. MY ARKANSAN BROTHER-IN-LAW OFTEN MAKES GIFTS OF PEPPER SAUCE, AND THIS IS HIS RECIPE. AT FIRST THE PEPPERS WILL BE BRILLIANT GREEN, BUT THE VINEGAR QUICKLY BLEACHES THEM. ❀ YOU WILL NEED A BOTTLE WITH A NARROW NECK SO THAT YOU CAN SHAKE OUT THE VINEGAR. WORCESTERSHIRE, SOY, OR STEAK SAUCE BOTTLES, AS WELL AS VINEGAR BOTTLES, SERVE ESPECIALLY WELL. A 2-CUP BOTTLE WILL WORK FOR THE PROPORTIONS GIVEN HERE. YOU'LL ALSO NEED ENOUGH SMALL, FRESH, HOT CHILE PEPPERS TO FILL THE BOTTLE—THEY CAN BE JALAPEÑOS, SERRANOS, CAYENNES, OR TABASCOS, AND RED, GREEN, OR A MIX. JUST BE SURE THEY'RE NICE AND FRESH AND AREN'T TOO CURVY.

Drop the peppers into a clean bottle. Heat the vinegar to near boiling, then pour as much of it into the bottle as will fit. Let the bottle stand, uncapped, until cool. The peppers will absorb some of the vinegar. Add the remaining vinegar to fill the bottle, then cap and set aside in a cupboard. The vinegar will be ready to use in 6 weeks and will keep indefinitely.

4 ounces small, fresh, hot chiles

1 cup distilled or white wine vinegar, plus more

chapter two

SOUPS, SALADS, AND SANDWICHES

SOUPS, SALADS, AND SANDWICHES

A BOWL OF SOUP AND A SANDWICH, A SANDWICH WITH A SALAD, SOUP AND SALAD — AMERICANS PAIR THESE DISHES IN EVERY POSSIBLE COMBINATION AND ARE OFTEN CONTENT WITH ONE OF THEM FOR LUNCH OR A LIGHT SUPPER. These good foods are easy to make without meat. Indeed, many of them are really old-fashioned vegetarian dishes.

SOUPS

THERE IS A GREAT REPERTOIRE OF AMERICAN SOUPS THAT WE HAVE A READY AFFECTION FOR, IN PART BECAUSE THEY'VE BEEN WITH US A LONG TIME. Many traditional soups were extremely hearty and based on large amounts of meat—a far cry from today's lighter, vegetable-centered concoctions. But there are countless chowders, stews, potages, and bisques that are easily made without meat or poultry.

Soup makes a wholesome, economical, nourishing meal that's often filling yet not calorie laden. It can also start a meal or, as is frequently the case, be paired with a sandwich. Soups are appropriate in all seasons and many can be made with water or a simple vegetable stock (page 29). Classic American bean soups always call for a ham bone or other piece of pork, although vegetarians have learned to do without the smoky, fatty flavor that these additions offer. But their presence does point to the importance of including some fat with our beans and legumes. Today, however, that distinctive flavor is just as likely to be imparted by olive oil.

BASIC VEGETABLE STOCK

MAKES ABOUT 6 CUPS

OU CAN TAILOR THIS BASIC STOCK TO THE DISH YOU'RE MAKING BY INCLUDING ANY TRIMMINGS FROM THE VEGETABLES YOU'RE USING AND ANY HERBS AND SPICES THAT ARE APPROPRIATE.

Warm the oil in a wide soup pot over medium heat. Add the onion, carrots, celery, green onions, mushrooms (if using), yeast, and bay leaves. Cook, stirring frequently, for 10 to 15 minutes The more color the vegetables get, the richer the flavor of the stock. Add the remaining ingredients and bring to a boil. Simmer, uncovered, for 45 minutes, then strain into a bowl. Use right away, or let cool, then cover and refrigerate. It will keep for up to a week.

1 to 2 tablespoons olive oil or
   vegetable oil

1 large yellow onion, chopped

2 carrots, thinly sliced

2 celery stalks, including a few leaves,
   chopped

1 bunch green onions, including half of
   the greens, chopped

a few chopped mushrooms (optional)

1 tablespoon nutritional yeast

2 bay leaves

6 thyme sprigs, or ½ teaspoon dried
   thyme

8 cloves garlic, crushed but unpeeled

10 parsley sprigs

2 teaspoons salt

10 peppercorns

2½ quarts water

CORN CHOWDER

SERVES 4 TO 6

THE CLASSIC AMERICAN CORN CHOWDER IS A SUMMER STEW OF SWEET LEEKS, NEW POTATOES, FRESH CORN, AND MILK. SALSIFY, AN OLD-FASHIONED ROOT VEGETABLE ALSO KNOWN AS OYSTER PLANT, IS SOMETIMES MENTIONED AS AN INGREDIENT, AND IT IS ASSUREDLY DELICIOUS IF IT CAN BE TRACKED DOWN. CHOWDER MAKES A FINE DINNER WHEN APPETITES ARE LIGHT. A LITTLE CHOPPED PARSLEY BRIGHTENS ITS LOOK, BUT MANY HERBS GO WELL WITH CORN — BASIL, CHIVES, LOVAGE, THYME. IN FACT, AN HERB BUTTER SWIRLED INTO THE HOT SOUP MAKES A SPLENDID AROMATIC FINISH.

3 tablespoons butter

2 small leeks, white part only, or
    1 yellow onion, finely chopped

3 thyme sprigs

4 small new potatoes, peeled and cut
    into small dice

4 cups water

5 ears of fresh sweet corn,
    white or yellow

3 cups milk

1 teaspoon salt, or to taste

freshly ground pepper

chopped herbs or snipped chives (see note)

If using chopped leeks, rinse them well to rid them of any sand and grit. Melt the butter in a soup pot over medium heat, add the leeks or onion and thyme, and cook for 3 or 4 minutes. Add the potatoes and water and bring to a boil. Lower the heat, cover, and simmer until the potatoes are tender, about 15 minutes.

While the potatoes are cooking, shuck the corn and pull off the silks. Holding an ear stem end down in a deep bowl and using a sharp knife, slice the kernels off the corn, removing just the tops. Then turn your knife over and, using the dull side, press it down the length of the cob, squeezing out the rest of the corn and the milk. Repeat with the remaining ears.

Add the corn to the pot along with the milk and bring to a boil. Lower the heat and simmer for 15 minutes. Add the salt and the pepper to taste. Serve with the chopped herbs or snipped chives scattered over the top.

BOSTON BLACK BEAN SOUP

SERVES 6

WE ASSOCIATE BLACK BEANS SO THOROUGHLY WITH THE SOUTHWEST NOW THAT WE FORGET THEY WERE FIRST POPULAR ON THE EASTERN SEABOARD AND ARE A RELATIVELY NEW ADDITION TO THE SOUTHWESTERN PANTRY. A FRIEND, WHO GREW UP IN A NORTHERN NEW MEXICAN VILLAGE TOLD ME THAT HE REMEMBERED EATING BLACK BEANS AS A CHILD, A VERY SURPRISING MEMORY IN A STATE WHERE THE PINTO IS CLEARLY FAVORED. IT TURNED OUT THAT HIS MOTHER HAD HAD A PEN PAL IN THE EAST WHEN SHE WAS A GIRL, AND ONCE A YEAR THEY EXCHANGED PACKAGES OF BEANS — BLACK BEANS AND PINTOS. ❀ THIS BOSTON SOUP AND OTHER REGIONAL VARIATIONS, SUCH AS PHILADELPHIA BLACK BEAN SOUP, SHOW UP IN COMMUNITY RECIPE BOOKS ALL ALONG THE ATLANTIC SEABOARD. A ROUX AND CREAM WERE USED TO THICKEN THIS SOUP, ELEMENTS THAT DON'T SEEM A PART OF CULINARY SENSIBILITIES NOW, NOR ARE THEY NECESSARY. THE SOUP HAS PLENTY OF BODY WITHOUT THEM.

Rinse the beans and set them aside. In a wide soup pot over medium heat, melt the butter and add the onion, bay leaves, celery, and garlic. Cook, stirring occasionally, until the onion has browned around the edges, about 5 minutes. Stir in the mustard and ground cloves, add the beans and water, and bring to a boil. Lower the heat, cover partially, and cook at a gentle boil until the beans are soft but not quite done, about 45 minutes. Add the salt and continue to cook until the beans are fully tender, about 30 minutes more.

Let cool briefly, then, working in batches if necessary, purée in a blender until smooth. Return to the pot, stir in the half-and-half, and season to taste with pepper and lemon juice. Reheat to serving temperature.

To serve, lay a clove-pierced lemon slice on each bowl of soup, and scatter the parsley and diced egg over the top.

1½ cups dried black beans, picked over
    and soaked overnight in water to
    cover

3 tablespoons butter

1 cup finely chopped yellow onion

2 bay leaves

½ cup diced celery

2 teaspoons minced garlic

1½ teaspoons dry mustard

¼ teaspoon ground cloves

2 quarts water

1 tablespoon salt

1 cup half-and half or milk

freshly ground pepper

fresh lemon juice to taste
    (about 4 teaspoons)

6 lemon slices, each pierced with a clove

2 tablespoons chopped parsley

1 hard-cooked egg, diced

JERUSALEM ARTICHOKE BISQUE

SERVES 4 TO 6

THE TUBERS OF THE PROLIFIC SUNFLOWER WERE ONE OF THE NEW WORLD FOODS THAT FED THE EARLY SETTLERS BEFORE THEIR OWN GARDENS WERE ESTABLISHED. DESPITE THEIR LONG HISTORY, THESE NUTTY TUBERS ARE NOT CONSUMED AS MUCH AS THEY ONCE WERE. CALLED BOTH JERUSALEM ARTICHOKES AND SUNCHOKES, THEIR FLAVOR IS EARTHY, YET SWEET, SOMETHING LIKE WATER CHEST-NUTS OR JICAMA. THEY CAN BE EATEN AS A SALAD, PICKLED, ROASTED OR BAKED, OR MADE INTO SOUPS AND STEWS. THIS BISQUE IS AN EXCELLENT WAY TO SHOWCASE THEIR DELICATE FLAVOR.

1 pound Jerusalem artichokes

3 tablespoons butter

1 yellow onion or 2 leeks, white part only, thinly sliced

1 small potato, peeled and diced

1 tablespoon flour

6 cups Vegetable Stock (page 29)

salt and freshly ground pepper

few gratings of nutmeg

½ cup light cream (optional)

½ cup small croutons, made from white or whole-wheat bread

¼ cup finely chopped watercress leaves

Scrub the Jerusalem artichokes but do not peel; slice them into ¼-inch-thick rounds. In a wide soup pot over medium heat, melt 2 tablespoons of the butter, add the artichokes, onion or leeks, and potato. Cook until the onion or leeks are limp, about 5 minutes. Stir in the flour and cook for a minute or so, then add the stock and bring it to a boil. Lower the heat and simmer, partially covered, until the vegetables are soft, about 25 minutes.

Let cool briefly, then purée in a blender, in batches if necessary, and pass through a sieve set over a clean saucepan so that it's perfectly smooth. Season to taste with salt, pepper, and nutmeg, then stir in the cream, if using, and return to the stove until hot.

Meanwhile, in a skillet over medium heat, brown the croutons in the remaining 1 tablespoon butter. Ladle the soup into bowls, scatter the watercress over the top, and add the croutons or pass them separately.

PINE NUT AND CHICK-PEA SOUP WITH MINT

SERVES 4

PINE NUTS ARE INDIGENOUS TO THE SOUTHWEST, AND THE SPANISH WHO SETTLED THERE HAVE LONG CULTIVATED THE CHICK-PEA. THERE ARE OLD RECIPES FOR PINE NUT SOUPS, CHICK-PEA SOUPS, AND FOR ONE THAT COMBINES THEM—A GOOD IDEA, FOR PINE NUTS ARE VERY EXPENSIVE AND EXTREMELY RICH. (YOU CAN ALSO MAKE THIS WITH SUNFLOWER OR PUMPKIN SEEDS.) TRADITIONALLY, THIS SOUP WOULD BE MADE WITH A BEEF STOCK, BUT USING WATER OR VEGETABLE STOCK KEEPS THE DELICATE FLAVOR OF THE PINE NUTS FROM BEING OVERWHELMED.

Melt the butter in a soup pot with the oil. Add the onions, garlic, celery, sage, and pine nuts and cook over medium heat, stirring occasionally, until the onions are limp and the pine nuts have browned, about 10 minutes. Add the chick-peas, water or stock, and 1½ teaspoons salt and bring to a boil. Lower the heat, cover, and simmer over medium-low heat for 15 minutes.

Let cool briefly, then, working in batches if necessary, purée in a blender until smooth. Return the soup to the pot, stir in the mint and slowly reheat so that the mint can steep for a few minutes. Taste for salt, season with pepper, and serve.

1 teaspoon butter

2 teaspoons sunflower seed oil

1 cup sliced yellow onions

1 small clove garlic, crushed

1 celery stalk, chopped

2 sage leaves, roughly chopped

½ cup pine nuts

1 cup drained canned or freshly cooked
    chick-peas

4 cups water or Vegetable Stock
    (page 29)

salt and freshly ground pepper

2 tablespoons chopped mint

CREAM OF TOMATO SOUP

SERVES 4

THIS SOUP RESULTS FROM HAVING JARS OF CANNED TOMATOES IN THE PANTRY, FOR NO ONE WANTS TO EAT HOT SOUP WHEN TOMATOES ARE IN SEASON, AND THE FRESH ONES AVAILABLE IN WINTER ARE HARDLY SUITABLE. INDEED, TOMATO BISQUES WERE CROPPING UP IN COMMUNITY COOKBOOKS LONG BEFORE WINTER TOMATOES GARNERED THEIR BAD REPUTATION. FORTUNATELY, EXCELLENT ORGANIC CANNED TOMATOES ARE AVAILABLE FOR TODAY'S SOUP. CREAM OF TOMATO SOUP AND A CHEESE DREAM (PAGE 57) WAS LUNCH IN THE FIFTIES WHEN SCHOOL KIDS STILL WENT HOME TO EAT. IF YOU EAT LUNCH AT HOME, TRY IT—IT'S STILL GREAT.

2½ tablespoons butter

½ cup diced celery

½ cup diced yellow onion

pinch of ground cloves

1½ teaspoons dried basil, crushed
    between your fingers

2 tablespoons flour

2 cans (15 ounces each) diced tomatoes
    in juice or in sauce

pinch of baking soda

2½ cups Vegetable Stock (page 29)

1½ cups milk or light cream

salt and freshly ground pepper

tomato paste, if needed

In a soup pot over medium heat, melt the butter and add the celery, onion, cloves, and basil. Cook, stirring occasionally, until the onion is limp, about 5 minutes. Stir in the flour and cook for a minute or so, then stir in the tomatoes, baking soda, and stock. Cover and simmer for 20 minutes.

Let cool briefly, then purée in a blender, in batches if necessary, until smooth. Return to the pot, add the milk or cream, and season to taste with salt and pepper. If the soup is too thick, thin it with additional milk, cream, or stock. If the tomato flavor isn't as rich as you'd like (if the tomatoes were packed in water), stir in a little tomato paste to bring up the flavor. Reheat and serve piping hot with a little pepper ground into each bowl.

SALADS

IKE SOUPS, SALADS ARE OFTEN LIGHT, FILLING, AND HEALTHFUL DISHES THAT CAN MAKE A MEAL OR OPEN ONE. It's easy to make good salads without meat, and there's a long tradition of vegetable-based salads that are perfectly suited to the vegetarian or the person enjoying a meatless meal. In fact, composed salads have long been popular dishes, particularly at ladies' luncheons of the past, but also in the nineties.

Many older salads, such as green pepper slices stuffed with sweetened cheese and covered with a mayonnaise-jelly dressing, seem strange to us today. Various tricks were used to make food eye-catching, including painting a pear with beet juice to make it red. When the refrigerator became widely available, molded salads of every hue and flavor were the rage. But among these oddities are many fine salads and dressings that have lasted over time: the Waldorf, potato salads, pears with blue cheese, coleslaw, the lovely Green Goddess dressing. These and others need only a slight tweaking to bring them up to date. One of the greatest differences between today's salads and those of the past would undoubtedly be the use of certain ingredients, such as olive oil for dressings and a bushel of new salad greens, from arugula and mizuna to red romaine and radicchio.

WOODEN BOWL SALAD WITH FRENCH DRESSING

SERVES 4 TO 6

I'VE ALWAYS THOUGHT OF THIS SALAD AS UNIQUELY AMERICAN AND WAS DELIGHTED TO FIND IT IN A 1913 REFERENCE LISTED AS "WOODEN BOWL SALAD." IT IS THE KIND OF SALAD THAT MIGHT BE SERVED BEFORE A MEAL OR ON A SPECIAL PLATE ON THE SIDE. IN HOT WEATHER IT MIGHT EVEN BE THE MEAL. WITH THE WEALTH OF NEW VEGETABLES AVAILABLE, FROM ARMENIAN CUCUMBERS TO CURRANT TOMATOES TO EASTER-EGG RADISHES, THIS SALAD CAN BE BOTH EXOTIC AND FAMILIAR AT THE SAME TIME. PICKLED THINGS—CAPERS, **PEPPERONCINI** OR ROASTED PEPPERS, OLIVES, ETC.—CAN FIND THEIR WAY HERE, TOO. THE FRENCH DRESSING HAS A CLOVE OF POUNDED GARLIC AT ITS HEART, A SUITABLY PUNGENT COATING FOR BLANDER LETTUCES LIKE ICEBERG.

Discard any ragged or damaged outer leaves from the head of lettuce and cut the inner leaves into bite-sized pieces. Wash and spin them dry, then pile them into a spacious salad bowl or into individual bowls. Arrange the vegetables, eggs, and cheese decoratively over the top, scatter the herbs over all, and season with salt and pepper.

To make the dressing, mash the garlic with the salt in a mortar until it breaks down into a purée, then add several twists of the pepper mill and the vinegar. Whisk in the oil, then taste to make sure the balance is to your liking. Aged vinegar is often too strong for the classic 3 parts oil to 1 part vinegar. Adjust as needed, to taste.

Just before serving, pour the dressing over the top and toss well.

1 head crisp iceberg or romaine lettuce

4 tomatoes

8 radishes, thinly sliced

1 cucumber

2 handfuls of sunflower sprouts

8 marinated artichoke hearts

3 large, firm mushrooms

3 hard-cooked eggs, quartered

12 long strips white Vermont Cheddar cheese or other favorite Cheddar

3 tablespoons snipped chives, basil, or marjoram

salt and freshly ground pepper

French dressing

1 large clove garlic

½ teaspoon salt

freshly ground pepper

1½ tablespoons aged red wine vinegar

5–6 tablespoons extra-virgin olive oil

CRISP ROMAINE SALAD WITH GREEN GODDESS DRESSING

SERVES 4 TO 6

IF YOU HAVEN'T ENJOYED THIS CLASSIC DRESSING, CREATED BY A CHEF AT THE PALACE HOTEL IN SAN FRANCISCO, IT'S TIME TO GIVE IT A TRY. CREAMY, THICK, SCENTED WITH TARRAGON AND CHIVES AND THE PRETTIEST SHADE OF GREEN, IT'S A FINE DRESSING TO USE WITH CRISP ROMAINE LETTUCE, TO SPREAD OVER TOAST IN A CLUB SANDWICH, OR TO SERVE AS A DIP WITH CUCUMBERS AND OTHER VEGETABLES. ANCHOVIES ARE PART OF THE ORIGINAL RECIPE; I'VE USED A CLOVE OF GARLIC TO PROVIDE A DIFFERENT BITE, AND WHILE NOT ENTIRELY AUTHENTIC, THE RECIPE STILL HAS A GREAT DEAL TO RECOMMEND IT.

Preheat an oven to 400 degrees F. Toast the croutons until crisp and lightly browned, 5 to 10 minutes, then remove to cool.

Combine the mayonnaise, sour cream, herbs, garlic, ½ teaspoon salt, vinegar, and water in a blender or food processor and blend until smooth and green. Taste for salt and add more, if needed.

Discard the outer, ragged leaves from the heads of lettuce and separate the pale, crisp heart leaves at the base. Wash and spin them dry, then place them whole in a spacious bowl. Toss them with enough dressing to coat as thinly or thickly as you like, from ¾ to 1¼ cups. Add the croutons and toss once more. Arrange the leaves on chilled oval plates and serve. Store the remaining dressing in a tightly covered container for up to a week.

1 cup small croutons, made from white bread

½ cup mayonnaise, preferably homemade

½ cup sour cream

½ cup chopped parsley

3 tablespoons chopped chives

1½ tablespoons chopped tarragon

1 clove garlic

salt

1 tablespoon tarragon vinegar

2 tablespoons water

2 small heads romaine lettuce

WILTED SPINACH SALAD

SERVES 2 GENEROUSLY

WILTING DANDELION AND OTHER GREENS WITH HOT BACON FAT IS AN OLD AND WORTHY TRADITION THAT SWEETENED AND SOFTENED THE BITTER EDGE OF HARDY WILD GREENS. IN THE CASE OF SPINACH, WILTING ALSO REMOVES SOME OF THE FUZZY FEEL THE LEAVES OCCASIONALLY HAVE. TODAY, OLIVE OIL IS LIKELY TO STAND IN FOR THE BACON GREASE. USE THE MOST TENDER LEAVES YOU CAN FIND AND REMOVE THE STEMS. THE GARNISHES NEEDN'T BE JUST WHAT ARE LISTED HERE. TRY PITTED GREEK OLIVES, WATER CHESTNUTS, TOASTED PINE NUTS, CURRANT TOMATOES, FETA CHEESE, OR THINLY SLICED BELL PEPPERS.

8 *thin slices baguette, brushed with olive oil*

4 *cups small, tender spinach leaves, carefully washed and dried*

2 *tablespoons chopped parsley*

2 *tablespoons chopped dill*

1 *tablespoon chopped mint*

1 *bunch slender green onions, white parts only, thinly sliced*

1 *tablespoon red wine vinegar*

salt and freshly ground pepper

3 *tablespoons olive oil*

2 *hard-cooked eggs, finely chopped*

Preheat an oven to 400 degrees F. Place the oil-brushed baguette slices on a baking sheet and toast in the oven until lightly browned and crisp, turning them once after about 10 minutes so they brown on both sides.

In a large bowl, toss together the spinach, herbs, toasted baguette slices, green onions, and the vinegar. Sprinkle with salt and pepper and toss again.

Heat the oil in a small skillet until nearly smoking, then pour it over the greens while tossing them quickly with a pair of tongs. Since the pan will be quite hot, you can pick up a few clumps of the spinach and swish them around the pan to wilt them further. Taste for salt and pepper, then serve, garnished with the chopped eggs.

TOMATO AND ONION SALAD

SERVES 4

T HE EAST, WEST, AND SOUTH ALL CLAIM A SALAD OF TOMATOES AND ONIONS AS THEIR OWN, AND NO DOUBT MIDWESTERNERS ENJOY THE SAME COMBINATION OF SEASONAL VEGETABLES. BIG, RIPE BEEF-STEAK TOMATOES ARE THE ONES TO USE, AND SWEET ONIONS, FRESH FROM THE GARDEN, IF AT ALL POS-SIBLE. SOME PEOPLE LIKE TO SLICE AND SERVE THEM RIGHT AWAY; OTHERS LET THE VEGETABLES SIT FOR A WHILE FIRST. SIMILARLY, SOME CHILL THE TOMATOES, WHILE OTHERS FEEL THEY'RE BEST STILL WARM FROM THE GARDEN. THIS TRADITIONAL STEAK-HOUSE SALAD IS USUALLY UNADORNED, BUT IF YOU HAVE A GARDEN FULL OF HERBS, THEY'RE DELICIOUS HERE.

Slice the tomato into rounds. Peel the onions but leave them whole, and slice them into thin rounds. Overlap the tomato and onion slices on a large platter. Sprinkle them with salt and a few twists of pepper and serve. Or drizzle olive oil lightly over all and follow with a few drops of lemon juice or vinegar; tarragon, red wine, and balsamic are all good choices. Leave plain, or garnish with fresh herbs scattered over the top.

VARIATION: Instead of slices, cut each tomato into 8 wedges, then cut the wedges in half crosswise. Chop the onions. Mix them together in a bowl and season with the salt and pepper and with the other ingredients, if desired.

2 large, ripe beefsteak tomatoes

2 sweet onions such as Walla Walla or Vidalia or onions fresh from the garden

salt and freshly ground pepper

extra-virgin olive oil (optional)

a few drops fresh lemon juice or vinegar (optional)

single chopped herb such as basil, marjo-ram, tarragon, or parsley (optional)

AVOCADO AND PINK GRAPEFRUIT SALAD WITH WALNUT VINAIGRETTE

SERVES 2

THIS SALAD COULD REPRESENT EITHER FLORIDA OR CALIFORNIA, SINCE AVOCADO AND CITRUS ABOUND IN BOTH PLACES. BUT USING A VINAIGRETTE MADE FROM WALNUT OIL AND ADDING TOASTED WALNUTS TO THE PLATE PLACES IT FIRMLY IN THE WEST, THE NATION'S WALNUT-GROWING REGION. ALMONDS ARE ALSO CULTIVATED THERE, AND THIS SALAD COULD BE JUST AS WELL MADE WITH AN ALMOND OIL VINAIGRETTE AND TOASTED SLIVERED ALMONDS. YEARS AGO ONE WOULD HAVE FOUND IT DRESSED WITH A SWEET POPPY SEED DRESSING, ONCE A CALIFORNIA FAVORITE.

⅓ cup walnut pieces

1 large pink grapefruit

1 tablespoon Champagne vinegar or
    white wine vinegar

½ teaspoon salt

1 shallot, finely diced

3 tablespoons walnut oil

1 head butter lettuce, or 3 large handfuls
    of arugula leaves, long stems removed

1 large or 2 small Haas avocados

Preheat an oven to 350 degrees F. Lightly toast the walnuts until they begin to smell good, about 7 to 10 minutes, then remove to cool.

Using a sharp knife, cut a slice off the top and bottom of the grapefruit. Stand the grapefruit upright on a cutting board and slice away the peel, following the contours of the fruit and removing the white membrane to expose the pulp. Holding the fruit in one hand over a bowl, cut along both sides of each segment to free the segments, capturing them and the juice in the bowl. Set aside.

Combine 1 tablespoon of the grapefruit juice, the vinegar, salt, and shallot in a small bowl. Let stand for 10 minutes to macerate the shallot, then whisk in the walnut oil.

If using butter lettuce, discard the ragged outer leaves, separate the inner leaves at the base, wash, and dry well. Gently tear them into large pieces or leave whole. If using arugula leaves, wash and dry them. Place half the lettuce or arugula in a bowl, add half of the dressing, and toss to coat. Divide the greens between two plates. Halve, pit, and peel the avocado(s) then slice crosswise onto a plate. Spoon the remaining dressing over the avocado slices then divide them between the plates, tucking them in between the leaves. Add the grapefruit sections and walnuts, and serve right away.

MELON AND CUCUMBER SALAD WITH BLACK PEPPER AND MINT

SERVES 4 TO 6

MELONS AND CUCUMBERS ARE CLOSELY RELATED BOTANICALLY, AND BOTH ARE COMPLEMENTED BY MINT AND PEPPER, SO THEIR JOINT APPEARANCE IN THIS MIDWESTERN SALAD SHOULDN'T BE ALL THAT SURPRISING. THE SLIGHT TARTNESS OF THE CUCUMBER AND THE SWEETNESS OF THE MELON PLAY OFF EACH OTHER, AND THE WHOLE MIXTURE IS QUITE LIVELY, STRIKING YOU WITH BOTH FAMILIARITY AND STRANGENESS IN EACH BITE.

Halve and seed the melon, then slice into sections. Cut the flesh away from the skin and cut into bite-sized chunks. Peel the cucumber, halve it lengthwise, and scoop out the seeds. Dice it into small pieces. Put the melon and cucumber in a salad bowl. Combine the mint, lemon zest, pepper, salt, and lemon juice in a small bowl, then whisk in the oil. Taste and adjust the balance, if needed.

Drizzle the dressing over the melon and cucumber and toss to coat. Cover and chill an hour or longer. Serve garnished with the mint sprigs and sprinkled with additional pepper.

1 ripe cantaloupe, honeydew, or other melon, about 1½ pounds

1 large cucumber

1 tablespoon chopped mint

½ teaspoon grated lemon zest

½ teaspoon freshly ground pepper, plus extra to taste

¼ teaspoon salt

2 teaspoons fresh lemon juice

2 tablespoons sunflower seed oil

mint sprigs

GERMAN·STYLE POTATO SALAD

SERVES 6 TO 8

ACCORDING TO MY FRIEND JODY APPLE, WHOSE FAMILY RECIPE THIS IS, "IT IS A GREAT, TANGY, CREAMY POTATO SALAD, AND ALSO MIGHTY SUBSTANTIAL." INDEED, IT COULD BE A WHOLE MEAL, BUT IS PROBABLY BETTER AS A SIDE DISH SINCE IT'S SO RICH. RED POTATOES HAVE THE KIND OF SURFACE THAT THE SOFT-COOKED EGGS WILL EASILY COAT, PLUS THE EGGS MAKE THE SALAD MOIST AND CREAMY.

2 pounds red potatoes

salt

3 eggs

½ cup chopped parsley

4 teaspoons sugar

⅔ cup finely diced white onion

1 cup finely diced celery

1 tablespoon apple cider vinegar

2 teaspoons mustard

1¼ cups mayonnaise, preferably
   homemade

¼ cup sweet bread and butter pickles,
   thinly sliced

freshly ground pepper

Put the potatoes in a saucepan with water to cover and add 1 teaspoon salt. Bring to a boil and cook until they are tender when pierced with a knife, 20 to 30 minutes. Drain them and let rest briefly to allow the outsides to cool.

Meanwhile bring a small saucepan of water to a boil. Slip the eggs into the water and simmer 5 minutes. Drain.

Peel the potatoes, cut them into 1-inch pieces, and put them in a bowl. While they're still hot, crack the eggs and spoon them over the potatoes. Add the parsley, onion and celery and toss well. In a small bowl, stir together the sugar, vinegar, mustard, mayonnaise, pickles, ½ teaspoon salt, and pepper to taste. Pour over the potato mixture and toss gently but thoroughly.

COLESLAW

SERVES 6

WHAT A LOT OF CHOICES THERE ARE WHEN IT COMES TO COLESLAW: RED CABBAGE, GREEN CAB-
BAGE, OR BOTH; CREAMY DRESSING OR TART; SPICY DRESSING OR BLAND. REGARDLESS OF STYLE,
ALL COLESLAWS BENEFIT FROM BEING DRESSED A FEW HOURS BEFORE SERVING SO THAT THE CABBAGE
SOFTENS AND THE FLAVORS MELLOW AND MERGE. COLESLAW IS GREAT ACCOMPANIMENT TO SUMMER
GRILLS AND PACKS WELL IN A PICNIC BASKET.

Put the cabbage and peppers in a spacious bowl. If stringy, peel the celery, then slice it. Chop up any celery leaves as well. Slice the green onions into rounds, and add the celery and onions to the bowl.

In another bowl, combine the lemon zest and juice, sugar, salt, pepper, mustard, horseradish, and celery seeds; stir to dissolve the sugar, then whisk in the oil.

Pour the dressing over the vegetables, add the parsley, and toss well. Cover and chill for 3 hours before serving.

VARIATION: Add a few tablespoons finely sliced lovage leaves to the coleslaw with the parsley and celery leaves. Just before serving, add 1 cup toasted sunflower seeds and toss well.

1 pound green cabbage, very thinly sliced

*1 green and 1 yellow bell pepper, seeded
and very thinly sliced*

3 celery stalks

*2 bunches green onions, including
1 or 2 inches of the greens*

finely grated zest of 1 lemon

2 tablespoons fresh lemon juice

2 teaspoons sugar

1¼ teaspoons salt

½ teaspoon freshly ground pepper

1 tablespoon mustard

1½ tablespoons prepared horseradish

1 teaspoon celery seeds

*⅓ cup sunflower seed oil or
safflower oil*

½ cup chopped parsley

PARSLEY SALAD WITH CHIFFONADE DRESSING

SERVES 4

PARSLEY SALADS SEEM CHIC AND NEW TODAY, BUT THIS SALAD IS BASED ON A RECIPE FROM META GIVEN'S **MODERN ENCYCLOPEDIA OF COOKING,** WHICH FIRST CAME OUT IN 1947. SHE REMARKS ON PARSLEY'S HEALTHFUL PROPERTIES, DESCRIBING HER RECIPE AS "A GOOD SHOT OF VITAMIN A." HEALTH IS ONLY A SIDE BENEFIT, HOWEVER, FOR PARSLEY SALADS TASTE WONDERFULLY FRESH AND INVIGORATING. THIS ONE WOULD MAKE A FINE STUFFING FOR A TOMATO.

1 large bunch parsley, preferably Italian

2 hard-cooked eggs

3 ripe tomatoes

1 plump clove garlic

salt and freshly ground pepper

¼ teaspoon paprika

2 tablespoons fresh lemon juice or apple cider vinegar

1 shallot, finely diced

⅓ cup olive oil, or to taste

butter lettuce leaves (optional)

Pluck the leaves off the parsley (they can be joined by the thinnest stems), wash well, and dry. Leave them whole or chop them roughly and place them in a bowl. Finely dice the eggs. Peel, seed, and finely dice the tomatoes. Add the eggs and tomatoes to the parsley.

In a mortar, pound the garlic with ½ teaspoon salt until smooth, then add some pepper, the paprika, lemon juice, and shallot. Whisk in the oil and taste to make sure the balance is right.

Pour the dressing over the salad and toss well. Taste for salt and serve mounded on a plate or in a curved leaf of butter lettuce.

WALDORF SALAD

SERVES 4 TO 6

SALADS MADE FROM CELERY GO BACK FAR IN OUR CULINARY HISTORY. THEY SHOULD PERSIST TODAY AS WELL, FOR CELERY MAKES A NICE CHANGE FROM OTHER VEGETABLES AND IS SO EASY TO PREPARE. THE WALDORF SALAD, CELERY MIXED WITH APPLES AND MAYONNAISE, IS THE BEST KNOWN, BUT THERE ARE OTHER WAYS TO APPROACH THIS FELICITOUS COMBINATION. VARIATIONS I OFTEN MAKE, SUCH AS USING GRATED KOHLRABI AND FENNEL ALONG WITH THE CELERY, WERE ALREADY MENTIONED FIFTY YEARS AGO IN META GIVEN'S CELEBRATED COOKING ENCYCLOPEDIA. HERE, A VINAIGRETTE INSTEAD OF MAYONNAISE AND AN ACCENT OF FRESH HERBS MAKE A PRETTY, CRISP SALAD FOR FALL AND WINTER. YOU CAN DRESS THE CELERY AN HOUR OR TWO IN ADVANCE, THEN TOSS IT WITH THE APPLES JUST BEFORE SERVING SO THAT THEY DON'T BROWN.

12 pecan halves

3 apples (use green and yellow ones)
  such as Jonagold, Golden Delicious,
  or Granny Smith

2 cups thinly sliced celery, pale inner
  stalks only

1½ tablespoons fresh lemon juice

1 teaspoon finely grated lemon zest

½ teaspoon salt

2 teaspoons mustard

⅓ cup olive oil or safflower oil

freshly ground pepper

3 tablespoons chopped pale celery leaves

3 tablespoons chopped parsley

1 head butter lettuce, separated into
  leaves

Preheat an oven to 350 degrees F. Lightly toast the pecans until they begin to smell good, about 7 to 10 minutes, then remove to cool. Break into large pieces and set aside.

Cut each apple into 6 wedges, but do not peel. Cut out the cores, then thinly slice each wedge crosswise. Place in a large bowl with the celery.

In a small bowl, stir together the lemon juice, zest, salt, and mustard, then whisk in the oil. Pour over the celery and apples and toss. Taste for salt, season with pepper, add most of the chopped celery leaves and parsley leaves and all of the pecans and toss again.

Line a shallow bowl or platter with the butter lettuce. Pile the celery in the middle and garnish with the rest of the herbs. Serve at once.

PEAR SALAD WITH BLUE CHEESE DRESSING AND ROASTED HAZELNUTS

SERVES 4

COMPLICATED LITTLE SALADS BASED ON STUFFED AND SAUCED FRUITS WERE A FEATURE OF LADIES' LUNCHEONS IN THE FORTIES AND FIFTIES. SOME SEEM A BIT PECULIAR NOW, BUT ONE THAT CAUGHT MY EYE WAS A WINTER NELLIS PEAR STUFFED WITH BLUE CHEESE AND COVERED WITH FRENCH DRESSING. WHILE THIS PARTICULAR SALAD MAY NOT BE THE ONE FOR US TODAY, THE ALLIANCE OF PEARS AND BLUE CHEESE IS HEAVENLY, AND NUTS COMPLEMENT BOTH. I SERVE THESE PEARS WITH ARUGULA, WHICH MAY ACTUALLY BE EASIER TO COME BY THAN THE GOOD WATERCRESS THAT WAS TRADITIONAL. BOTH ARE EXCELLENT. ANY EXTRA DRESSING WILL KEEP WELL, REFRIGERATED, FOR A WEEK OR MORE.

Preheat an oven to 350 degrees F. Toast the hazelnuts until the skins have begun to separate from the nuts, about 12 minutes. Remove and let cool briefly, then rub them in a towel to loosen the skins. Don't worry if not all the skins are fully removed—that usually happens. (If most of them adhere, send them back to the oven for another 5 minutes.) Chop them coarsely and set aside.

Finely mince the garlic with the salt, then put it in a bowl and stir in the lemon juice and the cheese. Mash the mixture with a fork until smooth. Whisk in the oil, the buttermilk or mayonnaise, and a little pepper, then taste. Correct the balance, if needed, with more lemon juice or oil. Set aside.

Peel the pears, cut them in half, and remove the core and the stem with a pear corer or a melon baller. Set them cut side down on the cutting board and slice them crosswise, at an angle, about 1/3 inch thick. Slide the knife under each half and transfer them to individual plates, placing 2 halves on each plate and fanning out the slices. Garnish the plates generously with the greens (or you can set the pears on the greens) and spoon the dressing over the pears and the leaves. Sprinkle the nuts over all and serve.

1/3 cup hazelnuts

1 small clove garlic

1/4 teaspoon salt

4 teaspoons fresh lemon juice

3 to 4 tablespoons crumbled Maytag or other good-quality blue cheese

6 tablespoons olive oil, to taste

1/4 cup buttermilk or homemade mayonnaise

freshly ground pepper

4 large, ripe Comice or Bartlett pears

several handfuls of tender arugula leaves or watercress

SANDWICHES

SANDWICHES HAVE A SPECIAL CHARM OF THEIR OWN. THEY REQUIRE SOME CARE IN THE MAKING TO LOOK NICE, YET WHETHER DAINTY OR HUGE, THEY ARE TRADITIONALLY PICKED UP AND EATEN OUT OF HAND. This strikes a fine balance between care and informality that tickles the food psyche.

Even though the sandwich, in one form or another, is a universal food, there is something about it that seems particularly American, especially when there is a platter of them cut on the diagonal and piled one atop another. Our sandwich know-how now includes the *panino, quesadilla, empanada,* Vietnamese salad wrapped in rice paper, *pan bagnat,* and the like, but there are some old-fashioned American sandwiches that aren't quite like any one else's, even though they may have originated elsewhere.

GRILLED CHEESE SANDWICH

SERVES 1

IT'S HARD TO FIND A BETTER COMBINATION IN A SANDWICH THAN CRISP BUTTERY TOAST AND SOFT MELTING CHEESE. ORANGE CHEESE WITH WHITE BREAD IS THE DINER STANDARD, BUT MANY CHEESES CAN BE USED IN THIS MANNER. TRY A MILD OR A SHARP CHEDDAR (SERVE THIS ONE WITH A GLASS OF APPLE CIDER OR ALE), CREAMY RICE TELEME (ADD FRIED SAGE LEAVES), A MILD SONOMA JACK, OR EVEN FRESH GOAT CHEESE OR CREAM CHEESE. WHITE BREAD IS PLAIN ENOUGH TO LET THE PERSONALITIES OF THE CHEESES SPEAK. BUT OTHER BREADS—RYE, WHOLE-GRAIN LOAVES WITH NUGGETS OF WHEAT BERRIES, WALNUT STUDDED WITH DRIED FRUITS, OR OLD WORLD **LEVAIN** TYPES—BRING A WHOLE NEW DIMENSION TO A TRUE CLASSIC. SERVE GRILLED CHEESE SANDWICHES WITH PICKLED CUCUMBERS AND ONIONS (PAGE 15), COLESLAW (PAGE 47), OR A CELERY SALAD.

Sandwich the cheese between the bread, using enough cheese to cover the bread nearly to the edge. Melt a scant tablespoon of butter in a small skillet. Add the sandwich and cook over a medium-low heat so that the cheese is soft by the time the bread is golden. Press on it a few times with a spatula while it's cooking. When the sandwich is golden brown on the bottom, turn it over, add another bit of butter, and cook the second side until golden brown.

VARIATION WITH TOMATO: Put a few slices of tomatoes between 2 layers of cheese.

VARIATION WITH MUSTARD AND HORSERADISH: Coat 1 slice of the bread, on the inside, with mustard and with horseradish, if you like its bite.

VARIATION WITH ONIONS: Thinly slice a small onion, then fry in a little vegetable oil until browned but some texture still remains. Season with salt and freshly ground pepper and stuff between 2 layers of cheese.

VARIATION WITH GREEN CHILE: Roast a long, green chile over an open flame or in a broiler until blistered; place in a covered bowl for 15 minutes to steam, then remove the skin, stem, and seeds. Slice into long strips and place them between 2 layers of cheese.

VARIATION WITH SALSA: Drain off the juice from the Salsa (page 20) and spoon between 2 layers of cheese.

thinly sliced cheese (see note)
2 slices bread (see note)
butter, as needed

EGG SALAD SANDWICH

SERVES 2

ARELIABLE LUNCH-COUNTER STANDARD, EGG SALAD IS PERFECT SANDWICHED BETWEEN FRESH SLICES OF TENDER DILL BREAD, LIGHTLY TOASTED WHOLE WHEAT, OR A GOOD, DARK RYE. SOME PEOPLE LIKE TO ADD A DASH OF TABASCO SAUCE OR A FEW TEASPOONS OF FRESH DILL OR TARRAGON TO THE MAYONNAISE.

3 or 4 hard-cooked eggs

¼ cup mayonnaise

1 green onion, including 1 inch of the
    greens, thinly sliced in rounds,
    or 1 tablespoon snipped chives

¼ cup diced green bell pepper

¼ cup diced celery

2 tablespoons minced white or
    yellow onion

vinegar or fresh lemon juice, to taste

salt and freshly ground pepper

4 slices bread or toast (see note)

2 lettuce leaves

Peel the eggs and chop them finely. Put them in a bowl and add the mayonnaise, green onion or chives, bell pepper, celery, and the white or yellow onion. Mix well. Season to taste with salt, pepper, and a few drops vinegar or lemon juice to sharpen the flavor. Divide between 2 pieces of bread or toast, add a fresh leaf of lettuce—ruffly green leaf, red oak, crisp romaine, or even purple mustard leaves—top, slice, and serve.

FRIED GREEN TOMATO SANDWICH

SERVES 2

THIS IS NOT AN AMERICAN CLASSIC, BUT IT'S MADE FROM ONE — FRIED GREEN TOMATOES. THEY SEEM LIKE THE IDEAL SANDWICH FILLING TO ME. GREEN GODDESS DRESSING IS DELICIOUS IN THIS SANDWICH IN PLACE OF MAYONNAISE.

Slice the tomatoes about ⅜ inch thick. Coat both sides of the slices with the cornmeal.

In a skillet over medium-high heat, pour in oil to a depth of ⅛ inch. When hot, fry the tomato slices, turning once, until the cornmeal is golden and the tomatoes are tender but not mushy, about 10 minutes in all.

Toast the rolls and spread them with the dressing or mayonnaise. Layer the tomatoes, onions, and watercress on the bottom halves of the rolls. Set the tops in place, press down lightly, slice in half, and serve.

2 large green tomatoes

1 cup cornmeal, seasoned with salt and pepper

vegetable oil or olive oil for frying

2 sourdough rolls, sliced in half

Green Goddess Dressing (page 39) or mayonnaise

thinly sliced onions, preferably sweet ones

watercress or romaine lettuce leaves

CHEESE DREAM

SERVES 1

Essentially an open-faced melted-cheese sandwich, this was once the frequent companion to a lunchtime bowl of tomato soup at home. According to the late James Beard, fancier versions appeared in hotel tearooms where rashers of bacon were crisscrossed on top of the sandwich and pickles were served on the side. But this simpler version is the one I grew up with. The idea of the cheese dream is blissfully simple and suitable to an array of American condiments and cheeses, especially some of the new spreads like olive paste. And it does make a great soup accompaniment, or an appetizer to serve with drinks.

Preheat a broiler. Toast the bread and lightly butter it. Cover it completely with the cheese, top with a round of tomato, and season with salt and pepper. Broil until the cheese is melted and bubbling. Remove and cut into quarters on the diagonal or into fingers. Serve immediately accompanied with the beets or cucumbers and onions.

1 slice white or wheat bread
butter
thinly sliced sharp Cheddar cheese
tomato slice
salt and freshly ground pepper
Pickled Beets (page 14) or Pickled
*   Cucumbers and Onions with Fresh*
*   Dill (page 15)*

AVOCADO AND JACK CHEESE WITH SPROUTS

SERVES 2

FOR YEARS, THIS SANDWICH, ON WHOLE-GRAIN BREAD OF COURSE, WAS THE CLASSIC VEGETARIAN COMBINATION UNTIL WE DISCOVERED THAT GRILLED VEGETABLES AND ALL SORTS OF OTHER THINGS COULD BE SLIPPED BETWEEN SLICES OF BREAD. THE WORST EXAMPLE WOULD BE BURSTING WITH A THICK PADDING OF ALFALFA SPROUTS, THE TOMATO SODDEN, AND THE BREAD CUT ABOUT AN INCH THICK. YOU FELT LIKE A GOAT TRYING TO EAT IT. BUT IF THE BREAD IS KEPT A REASONABLE THICKNESS AND THE SPROUTS ARE FOR CRUNCHY FRESHNESS AND NOT FOR FODDER, THIS CAN BE A TERRIFIC SAND-WICH. TODAY'S SPROUTS ARE MUCH MORE INTERESTING, TOO. TRY PEPPERY RADISH SPROUTS OR BASIL, LEEK, OR SUNFLOWER SPROUTS FOR A DIFFERENT-TASTING SANDWICH.

4 slices cracked wheat or other whole-
   grain bread
mayonnaise
mustard
thinly sliced Monterey Jack cheese
1 small Haas avocado, halved, peeled,
   pitted, and thinly sliced
1 ripe tomato, sliced
salt and freshly ground pepper
sprouts (see note)

Spread the bread with mayonnaise and then mustard. Cover 2 slices with cheese, top with the avocado, then the tomato. Season with salt and pepper, then add a modest layer of sprouts. Top with the second piece of bread, cut in half, and serve.

DUTCH CHEESE SANDWICH FILLING

MAKES 1½ CUPS; ENOUGH FOR 3 OR 4 SANDWICHES

THE PENNSYLVANIA DUTCH AMERICANS CONTRIBUTED MANY RECIPES TO THE NEW NETHERLANDS, AMONG THEM COLESLAW, WAFFLES, DOUGHNUTS, AND THIS CREAMY, PUNGENT SPREAD, WHICH DESERVES TO BE MORE THAN HISTORY. (EDOUARD POMIANE, A NOTED DIETITIAN AND AUTHOR OF A NUMBER OF CLASSIC AND CHARMING COOKBOOKS, ENTHUSIASTICALLY RECOMMENDED A SIMILAR SPREAD FOR COCKTAIL SAVORIES.) COTTAGE CHEESE IS ONE OF THOSE STAPLES WHOSE VIRTUES TOO OFTEN GO UNSUNG. IT IS A DELICIOUS CHEESE, TANGY AND REFRESHING WITH ITS SOFT FINE CURDLETS OR CURDS AS LARGE AS POPCORN. ONE OLD AMERICAN RECIPE CALLS FOR SERVING MOUNDS OF FRESH COTTAGE CHEESE—HOMEMADE, OF COURSE—WITH A LADLE OF THICK CREAM. (HAVING BEEN RAISED IN PART ON A DAIRY FARM, I CAN IMAGINE HOW STUPENDOUSLY GOOD THAT MUST HAVE BEEN.) USE THIS CHEESE SANDWICHED BETWEEN WHOLE-GRAIN OR DARK BREADS, AS A SPREAD FOR CRACKERS, OR AS A DIP FOR CRUDITÉS.

If the cheese is very wet, pour it into a sieve lined with fine cheesecloth placed over a bowl and let drain for an hour or more. Beat in the crème fraîche or sour cream until thick and fairly smooth, then season to taste with salt and white pepper. Stir in the watercress, pour into a bowl, cover, and chill before using. (You can also whip it together in a food processor or blender and end up with pale green cheese.)

1 cup cottage cheese, any curd size
½ cup crème fraîche or sour cream
salt and freshly ground white pepper
1 cup watercress leaves, finely chopped

chapter three

HEARTY MAIN

DISHES

HEARTY MAIN DISHES

WHAT MAKES A MAIN DISH IS ESSENTIALLY TWO QUALITIES: SUBSTANCE — A MAIN DISH SHOULD BE FILLING — AND APPEARANCE — it has to assume center stage on the plate, one way or another.

Some of the ingredients that make a dish hearty and filling are protein and calorie-rich cheese, milk, and eggs. Those traditional main dishes that appeared as centerpieces at suppers or luncheons were often shy of meat but laden with these foods—foods that many people today are bent on avoiding. But Welsh rarebit, Cheddar pie, savory bread pudding, and spinach soufflé are a part of a slim legacy of meatless dishes, so I include them, to be enjoyed occasionally, or modified as one wishes.

Beans are protein rich as well, but much better for us, and a dish of red beans and rice, baked beans and brown bread, or hoppin' John can be arranged to look good on the plate. Molding the rice accompaniment in a tea cup is a simple way to give them the focus they need. Stews based on vegetables, such as gumbo or calabacitas, benefit by the accompaniment of toast or biscuits or some other defined-looking starch to set off their amorphous quality.

Croquettes and fritters made of lentils or potatoes also have strong stature on the plate and are filling, plus they can double as appetizers or small dishes. Stuffed cabbages or stuffed peppers are good starring players, too. And since casseroles have long been a part of our culinary heritage, we have, fortunately, a built-in tolerance for shapeless foods like tamale pies and pastitsio, as well as more stylish ones.

All these dishes are hearty and filling. Many are meant to be paired with a biscuit, toast, a tortilla, a popover, or something else from of our vast repertoire of breads and baked goods, accompaniments that complement them visually and in the mouth as well.

HOPPIN' JOHN

SERVES 4

Hoppin' John, black-eyed peas with rice, is the South's traditional New Year's Day dish that augers for a lucrative year to come. It's hard to make it right without that ham, but you can ensure that it tastes good by using some ground chipotle chile, which provides both the smoke and the heat that's called for. Serve with mustard greens tossed with roasted peanuts (see page 71) and a bottle of chile vinegar.

In a large, heavy saucepan over medium heat, melt the butter with the oil. Add the onion, chile, bay leaves, thyme, and allspice, and cook, stirring frequently, until onion is lightly browned, about 7 minutes. Add the peas and 4 cups of the water and bring to a boil. Lower the heat and simmer, covered, until the peas are soft, 30 to 40 minutes. When done, the peas should be juicy with sauce. Check the pan from time to time to make sure they are covered with water; add more if needed. Season with 1 teaspoon salt, or more, to taste.

Meanwhile, in another pan, bring the remaining 2 cups water to a boil, add ½ teaspoon salt, and stir in the rice. Lower the heat, cover the pan, and cook 12 minutes. Turn off the heat and let stand, covered, for 10 minutes more. Fluff the rice grains with a fork and serve with the beans and their juices.

1 tablespoon butter

2 tablespoons peanut oil

1 large yellow onion, finely diced

¼ teaspoon ground chipotle chile or
    puréed chipotle chiles in adobo sauce,
    or to taste

2 bay leaves

½ teaspoon dried thyme

pinch of ground allspice

4 cups fresh or frozen black-eyed peas

8 cups water

salt

1 cup long-grain white rice

BAKED BEANS AND BROWN BREAD

SERVES 4

BAKED BEANS, LIKE APPLE PIE, IS A DEFINITIVE AMERICAN DISH. THERE ARE A NUMBER OF SLOW-COOKED BEAN DISHES THROUGHOUT NEW ENGLAND, ALL WITH THEIR ARGUABLE DIFFERENCES. BUT THEY ALWAYS INCLUDE PORK OF SOME KIND, A SWEETENER—FIRST MAPLE SYRUP, THEN MOLASSES AND BROWN SUGAR—AND THE BEAN ITSELF, WHICH MIGHT BE A NAVY BEAN, MARROW BEAN, YELLOW-EYED PEA, OR ANOTHER. A SPLASH OF BOURBON OR RUM FINDS ITS WAY INTO BEANS AS THEY TRAVEL SOUTH. THE SLAB OF SALT PORK IS WHAT PROVIDES SUCCULENCE FOR THE BEANS. SINCE IT'S NOT USED HERE, I'VE SWITCHED TO THE SOYBEAN, A CREAMY, FAT LITTLE LEGUME THAT GIVES THE FINAL DISH THE RICHNESS IT NEEDS. SOYBEANS CAN TAKE UP TO 3 HOURS TO COOK UNTIL TENDER, SO I PREFER TO COOK THEM ON TOP OF THE STOVE UNTIL THEY'RE DONE, THEN FINISH THEM IN THE OVEN, INSTEAD OF TYING UP OVEN HEAT AND SPACE. UNSOAKED SOYBEANS TAKE 35 TO 40 MINUTES IN A PRESSURE COOKER.

3 cups yellow soybeans, picked over and
    soaked for 12 hours in water to cover

4 bay leaves

1 small yellow onion, peeled but left
    whole

4 whole cloves

3 tablespoons safflower oil

3 cups finely diced yellow onion

⅓ cup brown sugar

½ cup molasses

⅓ cup tamari soy sauce

2 teaspoons salt

1½ teaspoons ground chipotle chile or
    puréed chipotle chile in adobo sauce

Put the beans in a heavy saucepan with 2 of the bay leaves and the onion stuck with the cloves. Add fresh water to cover by 6 inches and bring to a boil. Boil, uncovered, for 10 minutes. Scoop off any foam, then lower the heat and simmer, partially covered, until the beans are tender, about 3 hours. Check to make sure there's ample liquid covering the beans while they're cooking.

While the beans are cooking, heat the oil in a skillet over medium-high heat. Add the diced onion and the remaining 2 bay leaves and cook until the onion is soft, stirring occasionally, about 12 minutes. Set aside.

When the beans are done, drain them, reserving the liquid, and place them in a bowl. Stir in the onion, brown sugar, molasses, soy sauce, salt, and chipotle chile. Put the beans in a shallow baking dish and add the reserved liquid plus water, if needed, so that the mixture is a little soupy and the beans are just covered. Preheat an oven to 350 degrees F. Cover the dish with aluminum foil and bake for 1 hour. Remove the foil and continue baking until the beans brown on top, another 30 minutes or so.

Serve the beans on plates or in shallow bowls. Present the bread on a board and if you wish to be traditional, cut it with a string. Otherwise, a serrated knife will do.

BROWN BREAD

A Saturday supper of baked beans always included a healthful brown bread that was once made all over New England, but is commonly called Boston brown bread. It can still be bought in cans, usually in the bean section of the supermarket. The long steaming is what gives the bread its characteristic texture, which is resilient and spongelike. The bread takes about a minute to assemble, but the steaming takes 3 hours of your unattended time.

To make the bread, combine the flours, cornmeal, baking soda, and salt in a bowl and make a well in the center. Pour the molasses and buttermilk into the well and then stir everything together. Add the raisins, if using.

Butter a 1-pound coffee can or 1-quart pudding mold and its lid. Pour in the batter and cover with the lid or, if using the can, with heavy aluminum foil secured with a piece of string. Set in a deep pot and add boiling water to come halfway up the sides of the mold. Adjust the heat so that the water burbles at a slow boil, then cover and cook for 3 hours. It shouldn't be necessary to replenish the water if the pot has a good, heavy lid. If not, check every 40 minutes or so to make sure there's plenty, and refill with boiling water, if needed.

When done, remove the lid and ease the bread out of the can or mold. Serve warm or at room temperature.

½ cup whole-wheat flour
½ cup rye flour
½ cup cornmeal
1 teaspoon baking soda
½ teaspoon salt
½ cup molasses
1½ cups buttermilk
½ cup dark raisins (optional)
butter for pan

RED BEANS AND RICE

WHEREVER BEANS ARE FAVORED, IT'S NATURAL TO PAIR THEM WITH RICE, SUCH AS BLACK-EYED PEAS AND RICE (HOPPIN' JOHN), BLACK BEANS AND RICE (MOORS AND CHRISTIANS), AND COMBINATIONS WITH NO SPECIAL NAMES, LIKE PINTOS AND RICE AND THESE SPICY RED BEANS AND RICE. THE STARCHY, SWEET BLANDNESS OF THE RICE SETS THE FLAVOR OF BEANS, WHICH IS ALWAYS UNDEMONSTRATIVE, TO GOOD ADVANTAGE. GRILLED SWEET POTATO SLICES, WEDGES OF ROASTED PUMPKIN, OR GOLDEN FRIED DELICATE SQUASH RINGS SERVED ALONGSIDE WOULD GIVE THIS SIMPLE FOOD THE VISUAL DEFINITION OF A MAIN DISH.

1½ cups red kidney beans, picked over and soaked overnight in water to cover

8 cups water

4 bay leaves

1½ teaspoons dried thyme

1 tablespoon dried oregano

salt

¼ cup safflower oil

5 celery stalks, diced

1 large yellow onion, diced

1 large red bell pepper, seeded and diced

3 cloves garlic, minced

½ teaspoon cayenne pepper

½ teaspoon freshly ground black pepper, or to taste

1 cup long-grain white or brown rice

2 tablespoons chopped parsley

Drain the beans, place them in a heavy saucepan, add 6 cups of the water, and bring to a boil. Skim off any foam, then add the bay leaves and half of the thyme and oregano. Lower the heat and simmer, partially covered, until tender but not quite done, 50 minutes to 1 hour. Add 1 teaspoon salt once the beans have begun to soften.

Meanwhile, heat the oil in a large skillet over medium heat and add the celery, onion, bell pepper, garlic, and the remaining thyme and oregano. Cook, stirring occasionally, until the vegetables are nicely browned, about 20 minutes. Add the cayenne and black pepper and season with salt. Add the vegetables to the beans and continue cooking until the beans are completely tender, 15 to 30 minutes longer.

While the beans are cooking, bring the remaining 2 cups water to a boil in a small saucepan. Add ½ teaspoon salt and stir in the rice. Reduce the heat to low, cover the pan, and cook for 12 minutes for white rice and 30 minutes for brown rice. Turn off the heat and let stand, covered, for 10 minutes more. Fluff the grains with a fork.

Scoop the hot rice into 4 coffee cups or ramekins, then turn them out onto individual plates. Surround the rice with the beans and their flavorful juices. Scatter the parsley over all.

BEAN AND SUMMER VEGETABLE GUMBO

SERVES 4 TO 6

NO CRAWFISH OR SAUSAGE HERE, BUT SOME OF THE ESSENTIAL FLAVOR ELEMENTS — THE DARK ROUX AND THE SEASONINGS — REMAIN, GIVING THIS VEGETARIAN GUMBO A LAYER OF ITS MEAT-RICH KIN'S DISTINCTIVE FLAVOR. THE OKRA PODS RELEASE THEIR SLIPPERY JUICES, WHICH THICKEN THE STEW. SELECT BIG, PLUMP BEAN VARIETIES, SUCH AS CANNELLINI, SCARLET RUNNERS, OR RED KIDNEY BEANS, FOR THEIR SUBSTANTIAL LOOK AND FEEL.

6 cups Vegetable Stock (page 29)

2 cups finely chopped onions

2 green bell peppers, diced into ½-inch squares

2 celery stalks, diced

¼ cup plus 4 teaspoons safflower oil

¼ cup all-purpose flour

2 bay leaves

1 teaspoon each dried thyme and oregano

½ teaspoon freshly ground black pepper

¼ cup chopped parsley

2 teaspoons hot paprika

1 tablespoon chopped garlic

¼ cup tomato paste

1½ teaspoons salt, or to taste

2 cups green beans

3 ears of corn

2 cups small okra, trimmed, and sliced

3 tomatoes, peeled, seeded, and diced

1½ cups cooked, drained beans

½ cup grated smoked Cheddar cheese (optional)

Make the stock, if using, then strain.

Toss the chopped onions, bell pepper, and celery in a bowl. In a heavy skillet, heat the ¼ cup oil until almost smoking. Whisk in the flour, then switch to a wooden spoon and cook over medium heat, stirring continuously, until the roux is a dark reddish brown, about 4 minutes. Turn off the heat, add half of the diced vegetables, and stir until the mixture is no longer sizzling. Set aside.

In a wide soup pot, combine the remaining 4 teaspoons oil with the rest of the diced vegetables, the bay leaves, thyme, black pepper, and parsley. Cook over high heat for a few minutes to sear the vegetables, stirring occasionally. Add the paprika, garlic, and tomato paste. Fry the paste for about 1 minute, then whisk in the roux and the stock. Bring to a boil, add the salt, and simmer for 15 minutes.

Add the green beans and cook 10 minutes more, or until they're soft. Meanwhile, shuck the corn and remove the silk. Holding each ear upright in a bowl and using a sharp knife, slice off the tops of the kernels. Reverse your knife and use the dull side of the blade to force out the bottoms of the kernels and the milk. You should end up with about 2 cups of kernels. Add the corn, okra, tomatoes, and the beans to the simmering vegetable mixture and cook 5 minutes longer. Taste for salt. If you want a smoky flavor, stir in the cheese.

Serve the gumbo in wide soup plates spooned around a mound of white rice.

CALABACITAS

SERVES 4

CALABACITAS REFERS BOTH TO THE ROUND SUMMER SQUASH THAT'S STILL POPULAR IN NEW MEXICO, AND A STEW MADE WITH IT, ALONG WITH CORN AND ROASTED GREEN CHILE. THE SQUASH TASTES LIKE ZUCCHINI, WHICH CAN BE USED SUCCESSFULLY IN ITS PLACE. THIS IS A HUMBLE, BUT HIGHLY FAVORED DISH. MEASUREMENT IS LAX. IF YOU HAVE MORE CORN ONE TIME THAN ANOTHER, IT'S NOT IMPORTANT. A TRUE GARDEN STEW, THIS DISH IS CLEARLY BEST AT THE PEAK OF SUMMER.

First, roast the chiles. Place them directly over a flame or under a preheated broiler until the skins are evenly blistered but not too charred. Set them in a bowl, put a plate on top, and set aside to steam for about 10 minutes. Peel off the skins with your fingers, remove and discard the stem and seeds, and chop the chiles.

Shuck the corn and remove the silk. Holding each ear upright in a bowl and using a sharp knife, slice off the tops of the kernels. Reverse your knife and use the dull side of the blade to force out the bottoms of the kernels and the milk.

Heat the oil in a skillet over medium-high heat, add the onion, and fry until translucent, a few minutes. Add the squashes, corn, chiles, and salt and toss well. Cover and cook over medium-low heat until the squashes are tender, 10 to 15 minutes. Shake the pan a few times while the vegetables are cooking. Don't undercook. Cooking brings out the flavor of the squashes. Taste for salt and serve.

VARIATIONS: Add ¼ cup cream or crème fraîche to the vegetables when they're almost done and cook until it has reduced enough to coat them lightly, a matter of a few minutes. A scant ½ cup crumbled feta is also a good accent, as is diced Muenster or Monterey Jack cheese added to the vegetables at the last minute. If you like, add some chopped cilantro or parsley at the end.

2 New Mexican or Anaheim chiles

4 ears of corn

2 tablespoons corn oil or sunflower seed oil

1 white or yellow onion, finely diced

6 small zucchini or calabacitas, about 1¼ pounds, cut into ½-inch dice

½ teaspoon salt, or to taste

GREENS WITH ROASTED PEANUTS AND RED PEPPER

SERVES 4

FOR GREENS, YOU CAN MIX AND MATCH FROM MUSTARD GREENS, COLLARDS, AND KALE. I FIND A NEW GREEN THAT'S POPULAR NOW, BROCCOLI **RAAB**, HAS THE BITE OF TURNIP AND MUSTARD GREENS, BUT DOESN'T COOK DOWN TO SUCH A DEGREE. A SINGLE BUNCH WILL MAKE TWO OR THREE GENEROUS SERVINGS. CHILE VINEGAR IS AVAILABLE AT MANY SPECIALTY FOOD STORES. BOTH THE VINEGAR AND THE CHILES MAY BE USED IN THIS RECIPE.

Remove and discard the stems from the greens and chop the leaves coarsely. (If using broccoli *raab*, peel the stems, chop them into small pieces and cook them with the leaves.) Bring the water to a boil, add salt to taste, then the greens. Use a pair of tongs or a wooden spoon to poke them under the water. After the water returns to a boil, cook until the greens are tender enough to suit your taste, anywhere from 15 minutes to 2 hours, depending on where you're from. When done, drain and set aside.

Meanwhile, heat the oil in a skillet large enough to accommodate the cooked greens. Add the peanuts and fry over medium heat until they're lightly colored. Remove them with a slotted spoon to a paper towel to drain. Return the pan to medium heat and add the garlic. Cook for about 1 minute without letting it brown, then add the crushed pepper and the greens. Toss them in the oil and cook until they're heated through, turning them occasionally.

While the greens are heating, chop the peanuts and then add them to the pan. Toss everything together and taste for salt. Serve with chile vinegar on the side.

3 large bunches mustard greens or a mixture of greens (see note)

4 quarts water

salt

3 tablespoons peanut oil

⅓ cup raw peanuts

3 cloves chopped garlic

½ teaspoon crushed dried red pepper

chile vinegar

CAULIFLOWER GRATIN WITH CHEDDAR AND CARAWAY

SERVES 4 TO 6

VEGETABLES BLANKETED WITH A WHITE SAUCE APPEAR IN VARIOUS GUISES THROUGHOUT OUR FOOD HISTORY: SOMETIMES VEILED WITH A COVERING OF PARMESAN, OTHER TIMES CLOAKED WITH A LAYERING OF CHEDDAR, AND OFTEN CROWNED WITH A RUSTY DUSTING OF PAPRIKA AND BREAD CRUMBS FOR TEXTURE. TODAY, VEGETABLE GRATINS MAKE FINE VEGETARIAN MAIN DISHES. ACCOMPANY THIS ONE WITH WATERCRESS AND SOME PICKLED BEETS (PAGE 14).

2 cups milk

1 bay leaf

½ teaspoon caraway seeds, crushed or chopped

2 tablespoons grated yellow onion

1 large cauliflower, about 2 pounds

salt and freshly ground white pepper

2 tablespoons butter

2 tablespoons all-purpose flour

1 cup grated sharp Cheddar cheese

½ cup coarse fresh bread crumbs, tossed with 1 tablespoon melted butter

paprika

In a saucepan, combine the milk, bay leaf, caraway, and onion and place over medium heat. When small bubbles appear around the edge of the pan, remove from the heat and set aside to steep.

Cut the cauliflower into bite-sized florets; peel and dice the stems. Steam until tender-firm, 10 to 12 minutes. Without rinsing, immediately transfer the cauliflower to a buttered 8-by-10-inch gratin dish and season with salt and pepper.

Meanwhile, melt the butter in a saucepan over medium heat. Stir in the flour and cook, stirring, for 1 minute. Whisk in the warm milk, stir until it thickens, about 30 seconds, then transfer to the top of a double boiler and cook over simmering water for 25 minutes. Season with ¾ teaspoon salt and pepper to taste.

Preheat an oven to 375 degrees F. Scatter half of the cheese over the cauliflower and wiggle it in so that it falls between the florets. Pour the sauce over the top, fish out the bay leaf, and top with the remaining cheese. Scatter the bread crumbs over the top.

Bake until the cheese is melted and bubbling and the crumbs are browned, about 25 minutes. If necessary, brown the top under the broiler at the end. Dust with paprika and serve.

CORN-STUFFED PEPPERS WITH FRESH MOZZARELLA CHEESE

SERVES 4

STUFFED PEPPERS HAVE LONG MADE A SUBSTANTIAL CONTRIBUTION TO THE WINTER TABLE. WHILE MEAT FILLINGS HAVE BEEN REPLACED WITH HERB-SEASONED RICE AND OTHER GRAINS, THIS DISH GOES A STEP FURTHER. IT OFFERS A LIGHTER, SUNNIER VERSION, A SUMMER DISH MADE FRAGRANT WITH BASIL AND LACED WITH FRESH MOZZARELLA, NOW AN AMERICAN-MADE CHEESE. FOR PEPPERS, USE THE STANDARD GREEN STUFFERS, OR SWEETER RED OR YELLOW BELLS. SERVE ON A BED OF RICE, SURROUNDED WITH A SUMMERY TOMATO SAUCE.

If using green peppers, cut a 1-inch slice off the tops and pull out the seeds and veins. If using red or yellow peppers, leave the stem intact, halve them lengthwise, then remove the seeds and veins. Bring a saucepan of water to a boil, add the peppers, and parboil for 5 minutes. Drain, then rinse with cold water and set aside.

Holding each ear of corn upright in a bowl, slice off the tops of the kernels with a sharp knife. Reverse your knife and use the dull side of the blade to force out the bottoms of the kernels and the milk.

Heat the oil in a skillet over medium heat. Add the shallot or green onion and garlic and cook gently until wilted, stirring once or twice. Add the corn and the corn pulp and milk, raise the heat to high, and cook until the color changes in the kernels, 3 to 4 minutes. Season to taste with salt and pepper and stir in the basil, bread crumbs, and cheese. Remove from the heat.

To make the sauce, put the tomatoes in a heavy pan, cover, and cook over high heat with the basil. After 10 minutes, when the tomatoes are soft, pass them through a food mill placed over a bowl. The sauce should be fairly thin, but if you want it thicker, return it to the pot and continue cooking over medium heat, stirring frequently, until it is as thick as you want. Take care not to let it scorch. When done, season with salt and pepper, and stir in a few teaspoons olive oil or butter, to taste. (You will have about 2 cups.)

Preheat an oven to 375 degrees F. Oil a baking dish large enough to hold the peppers snugly. Stuff the peppers, set them in the dish, and bake until heated through, about 25 minutes. Serve hot or warm with the sauce.

4 green bell stuffers, or 2 red or yellow bell peppers

5 large ears of corn

3 tablespoons corn oil, plus additional oil for the dish

3 tablespoons minced shallot or green onion, white part only

1½ teaspoons minced garlic

3 tablespoons finely sliced basil leaves

½ cup fresh bread crumbs

1 whole fresh mozzarella cheese, about ¼ pound, finely diced

salt and freshly ground pepper

Fresh tomato sauce

2 pounds ripe tomatoes

3 basil leaves

salt and freshly ground pepper

olive oil or butter to taste

STUFFED GREEN CHILE CASSEROLE

SERVES 4

Proper chiles rellenos—green chiles stuffed with cheese—are batter dipped and fried, and are quite a production to make at home. This version uses the same ingredients, but skips the frying in favor of baking in the oven, which better suits the home cook. If you want to give the dish more panache, bake the chiles in individual casseroles, allowing two or three per serving. Poblano chiles, the dark green, glossy ones with wide, patchy shoulders, are favored for their heat and flavor. If you can't find them, use another long, green chile in their place, such as Anaheim or New Mexican. Serve stuffed chiles with rice and black beans or pinto beans.

12 poblano or other long green chiles
    (see note)
1½ cups grated Monterey Jack cheese
1 cup crumbled fresh goat cheese
    (about ¼ pound)
1 bunch green onions, white part only,
    thinly sliced
3 tablespoons chopped cilantro
½ cup all-purpose flour
butter for the dish

Tomato sauce
2 pounds ripe tomatoes, preferably
    Romas
about 3 tablespoons vegetable oil
5 cloves garlic, unpeeled
½ teaspoon dried Mexican oregano
salt

Roast the chiles directly over a flame or under a preheated broiler, until the skins are evenly blistered, but not too charred. Put them in a bowl, put a plate on top, and set aside to steam for 15 minutes. Slip off the peels. Make a lengthwise slit down the middle, leaving the stem end intact. Carefully remove and discard the seeds.

In a bowl, mix together the cheeses, green onions, and cilantro. Loosely stuff the chiles. If they fall apart, just wrap them around the filling as best you can; they won't show the patching in the end. Scatter the flour over a pie plate and carefully dredge the chiles in it, so that the batter will adhere.

Butter a large baking dish (or individual gratin dishes) and lay the stuffed chiles in it. Set aside.

To make the tomato sauce, toss the tomatoes with a little oil to coat them, then place under a preheated broiler or over a charcoal fire until wrinkled and charred in places, about 10 minutes. Turn them several times while they're cooking to expose all sides to the heat.

Meanwhile, toss the garlic cloves with oil to moisten and cook in a small covered skillet over medium heat until browned on the outside and tender when pressed, 12 to 15 minutes. Shake the pan frequently while they are cooking. When cool enough to handle, peel the cloves. Toast the oregano in a dry skillet until it begins to smell, then remove to a dish.

Purée the tomatoes and garlic in a blender until smooth. Heat 2 tablespoons oil in a wide, deep skillet. When hot, pour in the purée and add the oregano. Fry, stirring occasionally, until thickened, about 10 minutes. Season to taste with salt. Set aside and keep warm.

To make the batter, whisk the egg yolks, milk, oil, flour, and salt in a bowl. Set aside for about 20 minutes to rest. Preheat an oven to 400 degrees F.

When ready to bake the casserole, whip the egg whites until they form stiff peaks, then fold them into the batter; do not overmix. Spread the batter over the chiles and bake until the top is browned and the chiles are hot, 15 to 20 minutes. Spoon tomato sauce onto plates, and serve the chile casserole on it.

Batter

3 eggs separated

1 cup milk

1 cup all-purpose flour

1 tablespoon vegetable oil

¾ teaspoon salt

BAKED STUFFED ARTICHOKES

SERVES 2

THE ARTICHOKE HAS ALWAYS BEEN AN EXOTIC VEGETABLE, AND A FORMIDABLE ONE UNTIL ITS ACQUAINTANCE IS MADE FIRST HAND. THESE THISTLES WERE FIRST PLANTED BY ITALIAN IMMIGRANTS IN 1922, ON THE CALIFORNIA COAST WHERE VIRTUALLY ALL AMERICA'S ARTICHOKES ARE GROWN TODAY. IN THIS RECIPE, THE STUFFING IS FORCED IN BETWEEN THE LEAVES, SO THAT EVERY BITE CONTAINS SOME.

½ cup ground, roasted hazelnuts

4 medium artichokes

2 tablespoons olive oil, plus extra oil to finish

½ cup finely diced yellow onion

1 teaspoon minced garlic

⅓ cup dried porcini, soaked in warm water for 20 minutes

½ pound mushrooms, wiped clean and finely chopped

½ teaspoon salt

⅛ teaspoon freshly ground pepper

2 tablespoons chopped parsley

2 teaspoons chopped marjoram

1 cup fresh bread crumbs

¼ cup coarsely grated Parmesan or dry Jack cheese

water or part water and part dry white wine, as needed

Preheat an oven to 350 degrees F. Toast the hazelnuts until the skins have begun to separate from the nuts, about 12 minutes. Remove from the oven and let cool briefly, then rub them in a towel to loosen the skins. Chop finely.

Trim the base of each artichoke so that it will stand upright. Slice 2 inches off the top. Soak the artichokes in salted water for 20 minutes, then flush with running water. Steam, covered, over boiling water, until a leaf comes out fairly easily when tugged, about 35 minutes. Turn them upside down on a rack to drain.

Meanwhile, to make the filling: Warm the oil in a skillet over medium heat. Add the onion and garlic and cook, stirring occasionally, until limp, about 5 minutes. While the onion is cooking, drain the porcini, reserving the liquid, and chop finely. Add the porcini and the fresh mushrooms to the onion, raise the heat to high, and cook, stirring frequently, until the mushrooms have released their liquid and begun to color, about 7 minutes. Season with the salt, pepper, parsley, and marjoram and stir in the bread crumbs, nuts, and half of the cheese. The mixture should be moist and fluffy. If it seems dry, add some of the reserved mushroom soaking liquid and fluff it up with a fork.

Scoop out the chokes from the center of each artichoke and discard. Fill the cavities with the filling and then stuff the remainder into the base of the leaves.

Preheat an oven to 375 degrees F. Set the artichokes in a baking dish. Add water or water mixed with white wine to reach ½ inch up the sides of the dish. Drizzle olive oil over the top, cover with foil, and bake for 20 minutes. Remove the foil, sprinkle the remaining cheese over the tops and down into the leaves, and continue to bake, uncovered, until the cheese and filling begin to brown, about 5 minutes longer. Serve hot.

STUFFED CABBAGE

SERVES 4 TO 6

LIKE THE PEPPER, CABBAGES HAVE LONG SERVED AS STURDY, ECONOMICAL VESSELS FOR STUFFING. GROUND MEAT IS THE USUAL FILLING, BUT THERE'S NO REASON IT CAN'T BE A GRAIN. IN THIS CASE, A NORTH AMERICAN NATIVE, WILD RICE, IS FEATURED, MIXED WITH TOASTED WALNUTS, AND THE WHOLE IS BAKED IN A TOMATO SAUCE THAT IS SOFTLY SWEET AND SOUR. FRENCH RENDITIONS TEND TO PRESENT THE VEGETABLE WHOLE, WITH THE STUFFING IN THE CENTER AND IN BETWEEN THE LEAVES. GERMAN AND OTHER EASTERN EUROPEAN VERSIONS CALL FOR STUFFING INDIVIDUAL CABBAGE LEAVES. SOME MIDWESTERN RECIPES COVER STUFFED CABBAGE LEAVES WITH SAUERKRAUT AND TOMATO SAUCE, THEN BAKE THEM AS A CASSEROLE. IN ALL CASES, SAVOY CABBAGE IS THE VARIETY TO USE FOR STUFFED CABBAGE, IF POSSIBLE, FOR ITS BEAUTIFUL CRINKLED LEAF AND SWEET FLAVOR.

1 large head green cabbage, preferably
   Savoy or Dutch green

¾ cup walnuts

⅓ cup long-grain white rice

⅔ cup wild rice

salt

Tomato sauce

2 tablespoons olive oil

½ cup finely chopped yellow onion

1 teaspoon minced garlic

1 bay leaf

1 teaspoon dried oregano

½ cup white wine or water

1 can (28 ounces) whole tomatoes,
   with juice

2 teaspoons sugar

½ teaspoon salt

freshly ground pepper

1 teaspoon red wine vinegar, or to taste

To remove the leaves from the cabbage without tearing them, bring a large pot filled three-fourths of water to a boil. Cut the core out of the base, then submerge the whole head in boiling water for about 1 minute. Remove the cabbage from the pot and place it on a work surface. Carefully peel off as many leaves as will come off easily. Repeat as many times as necessary to secure 12 perfect leaves. When done, cut the core out of the base of each leaf and set the leaves, seam side up, on the work surface. Reserve the rest of the cabbage for the accompaniment.

Preheat an oven to 350 degrees F. Lightly toast the walnuts until they begin to smell good, about 7 minutes, then remove to cool. Chop finely.

Place each of the rices in a separate pan. Add 1 cup of water to the long-grain rice and 2 cups of water to the wild rice. Salt to taste and bring both to a boil. Lower the heat to a simmer, cover, and cook until the rices are tender. The white rice will take about 18 minutes; the wild rice will take about 40 minutes. When done, drain and set aside.

Meanwhile, make the sauce: Warm the olive oil in a skillet over medium heat. Add the onion, garlic, bay leaf, and oregano and cook, stirring occasionally, until the onion is soft, about 10 minutes. Add the wine or water and let the onions simmer over low heat 7 to 10 minutes longer.

Purée the tomatoes in a blender or food processor and add the purée to the onion, along with the sugar, salt, and pepper to taste. Simmer for 20 minutes, then add the vinegar. Taste and make sure the sauce is sweet or tart enough to your liking. Set aside.

Warm the vegetable oil in a skillet over medium heat. Add the onion, celery, and celery seeds, and cook, stirring occasionally, until the onion is limp, about 5 minutes. Add the garlic, toasted walnuts, parsley, thyme, and green onions. Season with salt and pepper. (You will have about 3 cups.)

Preheat the oven to 375 degrees F. Place approximately ¼ cup of the filling at the base of each leaf, just above where the stem was cut out. Fold the sides to make a neat package. Ladle enough sauce over the bottom of a baking dish to cover it generously, then place the cabbage rolls in it, seam side down. Cover with aluminum foil and bake until bubbling and hot, about 35 minutes.

Meanwhile, reheat the remaining sauce. Finely shred the rest of cabbage, then place it on a steamer rack over boiling water, cover, and steam until tender, about 8 minutes. Transfer to a bowl and toss with salt and pepper to taste and a little butter.

Place a mound of the cabbage on each plate and nestle the stuffed cabbage leaves in the center. Serve immediately.

Filling

2 tablespoons walnut, hazelnut, or
    vegetable oil
½ cup finely diced yellow onion
½ cup finely diced celery
¼ teaspoon celery seeds
1 clove garlic, minced
¼ cup chopped parsley
2 teaspoons minced thyme, or
    ½ teaspoon dried thyme
1 bunch green onions, including
    1 inch of the greens, thinly sliced
freshly ground pepper
butter

EGGPLANT CASSEROLE

SERVES 4 TO 6

Nowadays we might prefer to call this a gratin, a more elevating word than casserole. And this dish has the Mediterranean qualities to match the earthenware cooking vessel: eggplant layered with a stew of onions, peppers, and garlic, basil for the seasoning, and a bread crumb crust laced with Parmesan cheese. Instead of grilled meats, serve it with grilled polenta.

2 to 2½ pounds medium-sized globe eggplants

olive oil

2 large red onions, finely diced

3 cloves garlic, chopped

1 large red bell pepper, seeded and finely diced

2 large, ripe tomatoes, peeled, seeded, and chopped

10 large basil leaves, slivered or torn into small pieces

salt and freshly ground pepper

1½ cups fresh bread crumbs, made from country or sturdy white bread

¼ cup freshly grated Parmesan cheese

Slice the eggplant into rounds about ½ inch thick. If eggplant is in season, there's no need to salt them. Brush each piece generously on both sides with olive oil. Fry in a skillet over medium heat or cook in a preheated broiler until browned on both sides and tender, about 5 minutes on each side on the stove top or 7 minutes under the broiler.

While the eggplant is cooking, heat 3 tablespoons olive oil in a wide skillet over medium-high heat, add the onion and garlic, and cook, stirring occasionally, until soft, about 7 minutes. Add the bell pepper and tomatoes and continue cooking until everything is soft, about 15 minutes. Raise the temperature at the end of cooking to reduce the juices. Add the basil and season to taste with salt and pepper.

Preheat an oven to 325 degrees F. Lightly oil a 2½-quart gratin dish. Make a layer of eggplant in the bottom of the dish and season it with salt and pepper. Add one-third of the onion mixture, add another layer of eggplant, and repeat, ending with the remaining onion mixture on top. Cover the dish with aluminum foil and bake for 45 minutes. Toss the bread crumbs with a few tablespoons olive oil, to moisten. Remove the foil, scatter the bread crumbs and the cheese evenly over the top, and raise the oven temperature to 375 degrees F. Bake until the crumbs are nicely browned and crisp on top, about 25 minutes. Let cool 10 minutes before serving.

MUSHROOM STEW WITH GIANT POPOVERS

SERVES 4

ONCE A VITAL PART OF OUR PANTRY, WILD MUSHROOMS HAVE RESURFACED IN POPULARITY IN THE PAST FIFTEEN YEARS OR SO, AS AMERICAN CHEFS HAVE DISCOVERED THEIR CULINARY STRENGTHS. THIS STEW MAKES USE OF DRIED CHANTERELLES OR PORCINI, AND THEIR SOAKING LIQUID FLAVORS THE CREAM. CALLED DUTCH BABIES OR GERMAN PANCAKES AND USUALLY SERVED AT BREAKFAST WITH LEMON JUICE AND POWDERED SUGAR, THE GIANT POPOVERS DOUBLE BEAUTIFULLY AS A BASE FOR A SAVORY ACCOMPANIMENT. THIS COMBINATION IS SUGGESTED BY A MOTHER-DAUGHTER TEAM IN THEIR LITTLE BOOK **MOM AND ME**. THE WHOLE DISH, INCLUDING THE BIG, PUFFY PANCAKE, IS EASY TO PUT TOGETHER FOR A BRUNCH OR LATE-NIGHT SUPPER.

Place the dried mushrooms in a bowl, add the water, and set aside to soak. The chanterelles may need to soak at least 45 minutes to soften; the porcini should take only about 15 minutes. Drain, reserving the soaking liquid, and rinse them quickly to wash away any sand. Squeeze dry and chop finely. Strain the soaking water through a coffee filter or a sieve lined with a damp paper towel. Place the strained liquid in a small saucepan with the dried mushrooms, set over medium heat, and simmer for 5 minutes. Add the cream, a few pinches of salt, and a twist of pepper and cook a few minutes more. Turn off the heat and let stand.

To make the popovers, preheat an oven to 400 degrees F. Butter a 12-inch cast-iron skillet or two 9-inch shallow pie pans. In a bowl, beat the eggs until blended. Whisk in the flour a few spoonfuls at a time. Stir in the milk, salt, and the melted butter. Pour the batter into the pan(s). Bake for 10 minutes. Lower the heat to 350 degrees F and bake until puffed and golden, 5 to 10 minutes longer.

While the popover(s) is baking, melt the butter with the oil in a wide skillet over medium heat. Add the onion or shallot and cook until translucent, a few minutes. Add the fresh mushrooms, raise the heat to high, and sauté, stirring just occasionally, until nicely browned, about 7 minutes. Season with salt and pepper, then add the garlic and the cream infusion. Lower the heat and simmer until cream has thickened slightly, after a few minutes. Turn off the heat, but keep warm.

When the popover(s) is done, remove from the oven and slide onto 1 or 2 plates. Spoon the mushrooms over the top, then garnish with parsley. Serve right away.

⅓ cup dried chanterelles or porcini

1 cup hot water

½ cup heavy cream

salt and freshly ground pepper

Popovers
butter for pan(s)
3 eggs
½ cup sifted all-purpose flour
½ cup milk
½ teaspoon salt
2 tablespoons butter, melted
2 tablespoons butter
2 tablespoons olive oil
2 tablespoons minced onion or shallot
1 pound fresh mushrooms, wiped clean
*   and sliced ¼ inch thick*
½ teaspoon minced garlic chopped parsley

SPINACH SOUFFLÉ

SERVES 4

T HE SPINACH SOUFFLÉ HAS BEEN ON OUR FROZEN-FOOD SHELVES SINCE 1966—THIRTY YEARS. IT WAS CREATED FOR STOUFFER'S BY CHEF LOUIS SZATHMARY, ONE OF THE ORIGINATORS OF FROZEN DISHES, AND HAS LONG BEEN A FAVORITE OF THAT GENRE. A SPINACH SOUFFLÉ IS A WONDERFUL SUPPER DISH THAT CAN BE MADE EASILY AT HOME, TOO, AND IF YOU TAKE JAMES BEARD'S SUGGESTION TO LINE THE BOTTOM OF THE DISH WITH COOKED SPINACH, YOU'LL BE GETTING EVEN MORE OF YOUR GREENS. I ALSO LIKE TO ADD A LITTLE GRATED SWISS CHEESE TO THE SOUFFLÉ MIXTURE—PERHAPS ONE OF THE MANY SWISS-STYLE CHEESES THAT ARE MADE IN OHIO, WHERE, IN FACT, STOUFFER'S IS LOCATED.

Go through the spinach and throw out any leaves that are bruised or yellowed, then remove the stems from the remaining leaves. Wash the leaves in 2 or more changes of water until free of grit, then put them in a large pot with only the water clinging to the leaves. Cook over medium heat until wilted. If necessary, cook in batches. If cooking all the leaves at once, move them around with a pair of tongs to help them cook evenly. Drain in a sieve or colander, pressing out any extra moisture. Chop finely, toss with 2 tablespoons of the butter, and season well with salt and pepper to taste and a grating of nutmeg. Set aside.

To make the soufflé batter, melt the remaining 4 tablespoons butter in a saucepan over medium heat, stir in the flour, and cook, stirring frequently, for 2 minutes. Whisk in the hot milk all at once and cook, stirring, until the sauce has thickened and is smooth, about 5 minutes. Season with ½ teaspoon salt, white pepper to taste, and a few gratings of nutmeg. Place the yolks in a bowl and whisk in ½ cup of the hot sauce to warm them, then return them to the rest of the sauce and stir in the Swiss cheese. When the cheese has melted, stir in 1 cup of the spinach.

Preheat an oven to 375 degrees F. Butter a 6-cup soufflé dish or casserole. Coat the sides with the Parmesan cheese or bread crumbs, turning out any of the excess. In a bowl, beat the egg whites until stiff but not dry. Stir a quarter of them into the soufflé base, then fold in the remainder. Cover the bottom of the prepared dish with the remaining spinach, then pour the soufflé batter on top.

Bake on the center rack of the oven until nicely risen, golden, and mostly firm except for the middle, which may be slightly wobbly, 25 to 30 minutes. Serve right away.

2 bunches spinach

salt and freshly ground white pepper

6 tablespoons butter, plus butter for soufflé dish

freshly grated nutmeg

¼ cup all-purpose flour

1 cup milk, heated

4 eggs, separated

½ cup grated Swiss cheese

⅓ cup grated Parmesan cheese or fine dried bread crumbs

PASTITSIO

SERVES 10 TO 12

RECIPES IN AMERICA FOR MOUSSAKA AND PASTITSIO WELL PRECEDE OUR INTEREST IN MEDITERRANEAN FOOD, AND ARE FOUND WHEREVER GREEKS SETTLED. THEY DEPART SOME FROM WHAT TRADITIONAL GREEK COOKBOOKS OFFER. UNDOUBTEDLY FETA AND KASSERI CHEESE WERE, UNTIL RECENTLY, IMPOSSIBLE TO FIND. I'VE USED A GREEK RECIPE FOR A MODEL, BUT VARIED IT CONSIDERABLY BY REPLACING THE LAMB WITH VEGETABLES AND REDUCING THE NUMBER OF EGGS FROM THE DOZEN OFTEN CALLED FOR IN THESE DISHES TO A MERE THREE. ❋ PASTITSIO ISN'T HARD TO MAKE BUT IT IS INVOLVED AND USES LOTS OF POTS AND PANS. YOU'LL NEED A VERY LARGE CASSEROLE. I USE A ROUND SPANISH ONE ABOUT 14 INCHES ACROSS AND 3 INCHES DEEP, OR TWO SMALLER ONES. IT CAN BE ASSEMBLED AHEAD OF TIME AND BAKED LATER FOR A LARGE PARTY, OR BAKED IN INDIVIDUAL GRATIN DISHES FOR A MORE FORMAL PRESENTATION OF WHAT IS REALLY A RUSTIC DISH.

Vegetables

⅓ *cup olive oil*

1 *large or 2 medium yellow onions,*
finely diced

1 *cup finely chopped walnuts*

2 *medium-sized eggplants, 1½ pounds*
total, peeled and cut into small cubes

½ *cup dry red wine*

2 *cups diced canned tomatoes in purée*

1 *pound mushrooms, wiped clean and*
roughly chopped

¼ *teaspoon cayenne pepper*

2 *tablespoons ground cinnamon*

1 *tablespoon dried marjoram*

salt and freshly ground black pepper

¼ *cup chopped parsley*

salt

1½ *pounds penne or elbow macaroni*

First, prepare the vegetables: Warm the oil in a wide skillet over high heat. Add the onions and walnuts and cook, stirring every so often, until the onions begin to color around the edges, 5 to 7 minutes. Add the eggplants and mushrooms and cook, stirring occasionally, until they begin to brown and stick to the pan, about 10 minutes. Add the wine and cook until it is reduced by half, which will take several minutes. Add the tomatoes, mushrooms, cayenne, cinnamon, marjoram, salt and black pepper to taste, and parsley. Simmer for 5 minutes, then remove from the heat and set aside.

While the vegetables are cooking, bring a large pot three-fourths full of water to a boil, add salt to taste, and then add the pasta. Boil until it is just short of al dente; the timing will depend upon the type of pasta used. Drain and rinse well with cold water, then transfer to a large bowl.

To make the sauce, melt the butter in a 3-quart saucepan over medium heat. Stir in the flour and cook, stirring, until the roux is a light gold, about 4 minutes. Whisk in the hot milk, then cook, stirring, until it comes to a boil. Simmer for 5 minutes, stirring frequently, then remove from the heat. Beat the egg yolks in a bowl, then whisk in about ½ cup of the sauce to warm them. Stir the yolks into the sauce along with the cottage cheese and feta. Season to taste with salt and pepper. Remove from the heat. In a clean bowl, beat the egg whites until they hold soft peaks, then fold them into the sauce.

Add 1 cup of the finished sauce to the cooked pasta along with the feta, parsley, and cinnamon. Mix well.

Preheat an oven to 350 degrees F. Butter the bottom and sides of a baking dish (see note) and cover the bottom with half of the bread crumbs. Make a layer using one-third of the macaroni, then cover it with half of the vegetable mixture. Repeat with half of the remaining pasta and the rest of the vegetable mixture. Top with the remaining pasta, then pour the sauce evenly over the entire casserole. Dust with the remaining bread crumbs and all of the kasseri or Parmesan cheese.

Bake on the center rack of the oven until the top is golden and puffed and the pasta is heated through, about 1 hour for a single large casserole, 40 minutes for 2 smaller ones. Serve hot from the oven.

Sauce

4 tablespoons butter

5 tablespoons all-purpose flour

1 quart milk, heated

3 eggs, separated

1 cup cottage cheese, preferably small curd

6 tablespoons crumbled feta cheese

salt and freshly ground pepper

2 tablespoons crumbled feta cheese

¼ chopped parsley

pinch of ground cinnamon

butter for dish(es)

1 cup fresh bread crumbs, dried for 5 minutes in a 350 degree F oven or on the stove top

½ cup grated kasseri or Parmesan cheese

LAYERED BLUE CORN ENCHILADAS WITH RED CHILE

SERVES 6

IN SANTA FE, ENCHILADAS ARE USUALLY BAKED FLAT AND LAYERED, RATHER THAN ROLLED. WITH A FRIED EGG ON TOP, THEY MAKE A SOLID BREAKFAST THAT CAN CARRY ONE A GOOD PART OF THE DAY. IN A RESTAURANT YOU'D HAVE YOUR OWN STACK SERVED ON A PLATE, BUT AT HOME IT'S EASIER TO BAKE THEM IN A LARGE CASSEROLE. ENCHILADAS ARE ALWAYS BEST BAKED AS SOON AS THEY'RE ASSEMBLED AND SERVED FRESH FROM THE OVEN, BUT YOU CAN CERTAINLY READY THE COMPONENTS AHEAD OF TIME. LEFTOVERS MAKE A SPLENDID HASH. RATHER THAN CALLING FOR LARD, I'VE USED A GOLDEN, UNREFINED CORN OIL, WHICH REPEATS THE FLAVOR OF THE CORN IN THE TORTILLAS. THIS IS A RICH DISH, SO ACCOMPANIMENTS CAN BE LIGHT.

Red chile sauce

2 tablespoons corn oil, preferably
    unrefined

½ cup finely diced yellow onion

1 teaspoon minced garlic

1 cup ground New Mexican chile (mild)

1½ teaspoons dried Mexican oregano

½ teaspoon ground cumin

½ teaspoon ground coriander

4 cups water

1¾ teaspoons salt

1 tablespoon sherry vinegar

Enchiladas

6 tablespoons corn oil, plus extra oil or
    nonstick cooking spray for dish

10 blue corn tortillas

2 cups loosely packed grated Cheddar
    cheese, or half Cheddar and half
    Muenster cheese

To make the red chile sauce, warm the oil in a 3-quart saucepan over medium heat. Add the onion, cook for 2 minutes, then add the garlic and cook 3 minutes more, until the onion is soft. Stir in the chile, oregano, cumin, coriander, water, and salt. Cook 7 minutes, stirring occasionally. The chile will thicken the sauce. Add the vinegar and simmer for 5 minutes more, for the flavors to meld. Remove from the heat and set aside.

Preheat an oven to 350 degrees F. In an 8-inch skillet, heat the 6 tablespoons of oil until hot, but not smoking. One at a time for, fry the tortillas, turning them once with a pair of tongs, for about 6 seconds on each side. Don't let them crisp; they should stay soft. The oil keeps them from breaking down in the sauce. Remove to paper towels to drain.

To assemble the casserole, lightly oil or spray a shallow 2-quart baking dish. Spread ¾ cup of the sauce on the bottom of the dish and add a layer of 4 or 5 tortillas (cut them in half or odd pieces to cover the dish; some overlapping is fine). Cover evenly with 1 cup of the cheese and follow with another ¾ cup of sauce. Top with the remaining tortillas, overlapping them as needed, scatter ¾ cup of the cheese over the top, and then spoon over the remaining sauce. Sprinkle the remaining cheese over the top.

Bake until bubbly and the cheese is melted, 25 to 30 minutes. Serve bubbling hot.

MACARONI AND CHEESE

SERVES 4 TO 6

ONE OF THE FIRST DISHES BRIDES USED TO LEARN TO MAKE AND A PERENNIAL FAVORITE WITH CHILDREN AND ADULTS ALIKE, MACARONI AND CHEESE TRADITIONALLY CALLS FOR A SHARP ORANGE CHEDDAR, BUT WE MIGHT CONSIDERING VARYING THE STANDARD BY USING OTHER CHEESES. FRESH GOAT CHEESE, FONTINA, SWISS, AND GRUYÈRE—ALL MADE IN THE MIDWEST AS WELL AS ABROAD—COME IMMEDIATELY TO MIND. FOR THAT MATTER, THE MACARONI NEEDN'T BE THE LITTLE ELBOWS WE GREW UP ON—PENNE, WAGON WHEELS, AND OTHER SHAPES WORK, TOO. ESPECIALLY FANCIFUL ARE THE ECCENTRIC-LOOKING COLORED PASTA SPIRALS FOUND IN NATURAL-FOODS STORES. COOK A FEW HANDFULS SEPARATELY AND ADD THEM TO THE TOP OF THE DISH—THEY LOOK WONDERFUL! MAKE THE SAUCE AND COOK THE PASTA AT THE SAME TIME, THEN COMBINE THEM AND FINISH THE DISH IN THE OVEN.

butter for gratin dish, plus 3 tablespoons
*   butter*

salt

¾ pound macaroni or other pasta

2 tablespoons minced yellow onion or
*   shallot*

3 tablespoons all-purpose flour

3 cups milk (1% is fine), heated

1 teaspoon paprika, plus extra for dusting

¼ teaspoon cayenne pepper

freshly ground pepper

2 cups grated orange Cheddar or Swiss
*   or crumbled goat cheese (see note)*

1 cup fresh bread crumbs

Preheat an oven to 375 degrees F. Lightly butter a 2-quart gratin dish.

Bring a large pot three-fourths full of water to a boil, add salt to taste, then add the pasta. While it's cooking, melt the butter in a 2-quart saucepan with the onion over medium heat. Stir in the flour and cook, stirring, for 2 minutes. Whisk in the hot milk, 1 teaspoon paprika, and the cayenne. Continue stirring until thickened, then cook for 3 minutes longer. Season with the salt and pepper to taste.

When the pasta is almost done but still a little chewy, drain it, then return it to the pan. Stir in the sauce and the cheese. Turn the mixture into the prepared dish, cover the top with the bread crumbs, and add a few dashes of paprika. Bake until a crust has formed and the crumbs have begun to brown, about 30 minutes. You can finish browning the top under the broiler, but avoid overcooking—macaroni and cheese should be moist and juicy, not dry. Serve hot.

WELSH RAREBIT

SERVES 6

SHARP CHEDDAR CHEESE MELTED INTO ALE OR MILK AND SPARKED WITH MUSTARD AND A DASH OF TABASCO SAUCE, WELSH RAREBIT—OR WELSH RABBIT, AS IT'S ALSO CALLED—CAME TO US FROM THE BRITISH ISLES LONG AGO. I RECALL IT AS A SUPPER DISH, AND IN THE FIFTIES IT BECAME ONE OF THOSE POPULAR DISHES TO MAKE IN A CHAFING DISH, MUCH LIKE ITS RELATIVE, THE CHEESE FONDUE, WHICH SURFACED IN POPULARITY ABOUT THE SAME TIME. ONE ALMOST NEVER SEES WELSH RAREBIT ANYMORE, ALTHOUGH THERE ARE MANY VERSIONS OF IT IN COMMUNITY COOKBOOKS ACROSS AMERICA. PERHAPS IT'S THE RICHNESS OF CHEESE OR SIMPLY THAT SO MANY OTHER NEW DISHES HAVE APPEARED, BUT I THINK IT'S STILL A GREAT LITTLE DISH, ESPECIALLY ENJOYABLE ON A CRISP FALL DAY, WITH A WALDORF SALAD (SEE PAGE 50) AND A MUG OF CIDER. IT CERTAINLY COULD BE UPDATED, COOKED IN ONE OF THE NEW REGIONAL BEERS FROM A MICROBREWERY OR SEASONED WITH SMOKY CHIPOTLE CHILES INSTEAD OF CAYENNE, BUT THE ORIGINAL IS A FINE DISH.

In the top of a double boiler set over simmering water, melt the butter, then add the beer. When the beer is warm, stir in the cheese and keep stirring until it is melted and smooth. Beat in the egg, if using. Season to taste with salt and stir in the Tabasco sauce or cayenne and mustard. Some people like a few dashes of Worcestershire sauce, too. Serve spooned over the toast or muffins.

1 tablespoon butter

1 cup beer or ale

1 pound coarsely grated aged Cheddar cheese

1 egg (optional)

salt

¼ teaspoon Tabasco sauce or cayenne pepper

½ teaspoon powdered mustard

Worcestershire sauce (optional)

6 pieces toasted bread or English muffin halves

89

TAMALE PIE

SERVES 6 TO 8

I'S THE **MASA HARINA** THAT GIVES TAMALE PIE ITS TAMALE FLAVOR—THE ONLY LINK THIS DISH HAS TO ITS NAME. IT CAN BE FOUND IN MEXICAN MARKETS AND MOST SUPERMARKETS, UNDER THE QUAKER LABEL. LET THE **MASA** COOK IN A DOUBLE BOILER WHILE YOU'RE ASSEMBLING EVERYTHING ELSE.

Tamale topping

6 cups water

¾ cup masa harina

2 teaspoons salt

1 tablespoon ground red chile

2 tablespoons corn oil

Filling

2 tablespoons corn oil

1 yellow onion, diced

1 green bell pepper, seeded and diced

1 cup diced celery

2 teaspoons minced garlic

2 cups fresh or frozen corn kernels

2 cups frozen lima beans

3 cups cooked red kidney beans
(1¼ cups dried)

½ teaspoon dried oregano

1 teaspoon ground cumin

2 teaspoons ground red chile

1 teaspoon salt

1½ cups water

1 can (14–15 ounces) California black
olives, drained and sliced

1 cup grated Cheddar cheese

sour cream for serving

To make the topping, place the water in a saucepan and bring just to a boil. Whisk in the cornmeal and *masa harina* and stir until a boil is reached and the mixture is uniformly thickened, after a few minutes. Add the salt, chile or chile powder, and corn oil or butter, and transfer to the top of a double boiler. Place it over simmering water, cover and cook for 40 minutes while you make the filling.

In a large, wide pot over high heat, warm the oil. When hot, add the onion, bell pepper, and celery and sauté until the onion begins to color around the edges, 5 to 7 minutes. Add the garlic, corn, lima beans, kidney beans, oregano, cumin, and chile or chile powder. Add the salt and bean broth or water. Lower the heat and simmer until only a little liquid is left, about 30 minutes. Taste for salt.

Preheat an oven to 375 degrees F. Spoon half of the cooked cornmeal onto the bottom of a 2-quart baking dish and let it set for 5 minutes. Spread half of the vegetable stew over the cornmeal layer, then cover it with half of the black olives and half of the cheese. Top with the remaining vegetables and the rest of the olives. Stir the remaining cheese into the cornmeal mixture and spread it over the top of the casserole. (At this point, it can be covered with plastic and refrigerated overnight or until you're ready to cook it.)

Bake until bubbling and hot, about 1 hour. Serve piping hot with sour cream dolloped on top.

CHEESE AND BREAD PUDDING

SERVES 4

BREAD PUDDINGS HAVE ALWAYS BEEN POPULAR IN AMERICA, ESPECIALLY AS DESSERTS, AND THEY STILL STAND AS A SYMBOL OF THRIFT FOR MANY COOKS. TODAY, THEY'RE MORE LIKELY TO BE GIVEN THE ITALIAN NAME **STRATA** AND THEY CAN INCLUDE SUCH COSTLY INGREDIENTS AS CRAB MEAT AND IMPORTED CHEESES—A FAR CRY FROM THRIFT. BUT THIS OLD-FASHIONED SAVORY, MIDWESTERN PUDDING IS STRAIGHTFORWARD AND PRACTICAL, IF NOT ECONOMICAL. ALTHOUGH WHITE BREAD IS TRADITIONAL, I FIND WHEAT, RYE, OR DILL BREAD IS ALSO GOOD, IF NOT BETTER. SERVE IT WITH BAKED TOMATOES AND A SALAD FOR A BRUNCH OR SIMPLE SUPPER.

Preheat an oven to 350 degrees F. Lightly butter a 6-cup baking dish.

Spread a thin layer of mustard over the buttered bread, then cut it into fingers or cubes. Layer it, with the cheese, in the baking dish. As you go, season each layer with a dusting of paprika. In a bowl, whisk together the eggs, milk, cayenne, and salt. Pour it over the bread and cheese. Let stand for at least 30 minutes to absorb the custard. (Sometimes even soaking overnight is recommended for bread puddings.)

Dust the top with paprika. Bake on the center rack of the oven until puffed and golden, about 30 minutes. It should come out very tender, like a soufflé, which this dish was also called before real soufflés became known here. Serve immediately.

butter for dish

6 slices white, wheat, dill, or rye bread, a few days old and lightly buttered on one side

a few tablespoons mustard

1 cup coarsely grated Cheddar, Monterey Jack, or Swiss cheese

paprika

3 eggs

1½ cups milk

¼ teaspoon cayenne pepper

½ teaspoon salt

FRESH CORN PUDDING

SERVES 8

CORN PUDDINGS ABOUND IN AMERICA. EVERY COMMUNITY COOKBOOK—IT DOESN'T MATTER THE REGION—HAS AT LEAST ONE AND MOST LIKELY SEVERAL, ESPECIALLY THOSE FROM THE CORN BELT AND THE EASTERN SEABOARD STATES. THIS PUDDING IS THE ESSENCE OF CORN—SUNNY YELLOW, FILLED WITH SWEET KERNELS THAT BURST IN YOUR MOUTH, THE FLAVOR UNDERSCORED BY THE INCLUSION OF THE SCRAPINGS. IT'S FINISHED WITH A DUSTING OF MILD WISCONSIN COLBY OR MILD CHEDDAR CHEESE AND THAT UBIQUITOUS DASH OF PAPRIKA. MOST CORN IS NOW BRED TO STAY SWEET, EVEN IN THE SUPERMARKET, WHICH IS INVARIABLY SOME DISTANCE FROM ANY CORN FIELD. I PREFER YELLOW CORN, BUT WHITE IS CERTAINLY FINE. WHAT IS IMPORTANT IS THAT IT BE FRESH AND SWEET.

18 saltine crackers, or ¾ cup cracker
   crumbs or fresh bread crumbs
6 large ears of corn
1½ tablespoons corn oil or butter
1 cup finely diced yellow onions
1 teaspoon minced garlic
1 cup evaporated milk
2 eggs, lightly beaten
2 cups loosely packed orange Colby or
   mild Cheddar cheese
salt and freshly ground pepper
paprika

Preheat an oven to 350 degrees F. Lightly butter a 6-cup shallow casserole or gratin dish. If using saltines, put them in a bag and roll over them with a rolling pin to make coarse crumbs. There should be about ¾ cup. Set aside. Shuck the corn and pull off the silks. If you slice your corn in a deep bowl, you'll keep it from spattering all over. Holding an ear of corn stem end down and using a sharp knife, carefully cut off the top halves of the corn kernels; do not include the fibrous base, the part that gets caught in your teeth. Then turn your knife over and, using the dull side, press it down the length of the cob, squeezing out the rest of the corn and the milk. You'll end up with a mushy substance in the bottom of the bowl along with the kernels. Repeat with the remaining ears.

Warm the oil or butter in a skillet over medium-high heat. Add the onions and cook just until limp, about 4 minutes. Add the garlic and cook for 2 to 3 minutes without letting the onions brown. Add this to the corn and stir in the milk, eggs, 1 cup of the cheese, and ½ cup of the cracker crumbs. Season to taste with salt and pepper. Transfer the mixture to the prepared dish and top with the remaining cracker crumbs and cheese. Bake on the center rack of the oven until puffed and golden, about 45 minutes. Remove from the oven, sprinkle paprika over the top, and serve.

NEW ENGLAND CHEESE PIE WITH GREEN ONIONS

THERE IS A REPERTOIRE OF SAVORY PIES IN AMERICAN COOKING THAT RUNS A VARIED COURSE FROM SHEPHERD'S PIE, TO STEAK-AND-KIDNEY PIE, TO GREEN TOMATO PIES COVERED WITH MAYONNAISE, TO THIS CLASSIC. IT IS MORE OR LESS OUR VERSION OF THE QUICHE, BUT IN A VERY AMERICAN WAY, THAT IS, BIGGER AND DEEPER—A PIE, NOT A TART. USE A SHARP VERMONT CHEDDAR, OR BREAKING WITH TRADITION, A FRESH GOAT CHEESE.

Pie crust

1½ cups all-purpose flour

½ teaspoon salt

8 tablespoons (½ cup) chilled butter or
    shortening or a mixture

3 to 4 tablespoons ice water, or as
    needed

Filling

1½ cups grated Cheddar cheese or
    crumbled goat cheese

2 bunches green onions, including a few
    inches of the greens, thinly sliced

4 eggs

1 tablespoon mustard

2 cups milk, or 1 cup each milk and
    heavy cream

½ teaspoon salt

freshly ground white pepper

To make the pie crust, in a bowl, stir together the flour and salt. Add the butter and/or shortening and cut it in with 2 knives or your fingertips. Let the texture be coarse and varied, rather than fine. Sprinkle the water, 1 tablespoon at a time, over the flour mixture and mix with a fork. Add only enough water for the pastry to hold together when pressed. Gather the dough into a ball.

Lightly flour a work surface and roll out the dough into a circle 11 inches across. Carefully fold it into quarters, lift it into a 9-inch pie plate, and unfold it. Loosely fit it into the pan, then trim and crimp the edges. Put the lined plate in the freezer until ready to use. Chilling the crust this way will keep it from slumping when baked.

Preheat an oven to 425 degrees F. Sprinkle the cheese and onions over the bottom of the frozen pie shell. Set it on a sheet for easier handling. In a bowl, whisk together the eggs, mustard, milk (or milk and cream), and salt until blended, then pour through a fine-mesh sieve set over a bowl. Add a few grindings of pepper, then pour the custard into the pie crust.

Bake on the center rack of the oven for 15 minutes. Lower the heat to 300 degrees F and bake until the custard is set with just a small quivery spot in the center, about 30 minutes. Remove from the oven and let stand for 5 minutes, then cut into wedges to serve.

SCALLOPED POTATOES

SERVES 6

L OTS OF AMERICAN DISHES, ESPECIALLY IN THE MIDWEST, ARE SCALLOPED—SCALLOPED CORN, SCAL-
LOPED OKRA, AND THE BEST-KNOWN, SCALLOPED POTATOES, A VERSION OF THE FRENCH **GRATIN
DAUPHINOIS.** SOMETIMES "SCALLOPED" MEANS THE VEGETABLE IS COOKED IN MILK, AS WITH THESE
POTATOES; BUT OTHER TIMES IT INDICATES A COVERING OF CRACKER OR BREAD CRUMBS. FOR SCALLOPED
POTATOES USE WHOLE MILK TO ENSURE THE BEST TEXTURE, AND BE SURE TO HEAT IT TO PREVENT CUR-
DLING. SERVE WITH COLD APPLESAUCE (PAGE 19) AND A BIG GREEN SALAD.

Preheat an oven to 350 degrees F. Rub a 2-quart gratin dish or other shallow baking dish with butter and then with the garlic until it mushes into the butter.
Warm the milk in a saucepan with whatever garlic is left. Remove from the heat
when it comes to a boil.

Meanwhile, peel the potatoes and slice them into rounds ¼ inch thick or less.
Make an overlapping layer of potatoes in the prepared dish. Season with salt,
pepper, and nutmeg; dot with some of the butter and sprinkle with flour. Repeat
the layers until all the ingredients are used up, then pour the milk over all.

Bake until the liquid is absorbed and a crust is formed, about 1½ hours.

Serve hot.

*butter and 1 clove garlic, crushed, for
dish*

3 cups milk

*2 pounds Yellow Finn, Yukon Gold, or
russet potatoes*

salt and freshly ground pepper

freshly grated nutmeg

*4 tablespoons butter, cut into small
pieces*

3 tablespoons all-purpose flour

LENTIL AND ONION CROQUETTES

MAKES EIGHTEEN 2½-INCH CROQUETTES; SERVES 6

W E THINK OF THINGS LIKE LENTIL AND BEAN CAKES AS PART OF THE VEGETARIAN LEGACY OF THE SIXTIES, BUT SUBSTITUTES FOR MEAT, LIKE THESE CROQUETTES FROM AN IDAHO HISTORICAL COOKBOOK, APPEARED LONG AGO, WHEN MEAT WAS SCARCE AND NOT BECAUSE IT WAS A FOOD TO AVOID. IN A WAY THAT IS TYPICAL OF MANY EARLY AMERICAN RECIPES, THESE TASTY CROQUETTES DEPEND LARGELY ON TWO INGREDIENTS FOR FLAVOR—WELL BROWNED ONIONS AND THE LENTILS. A MORE UPDATED VERSION MIGHT INCLUDE ROASTED GARLIC, HERBS, AND PERHAPS COOKED RICE OR SAUTÉED MUSHROOMS, ALL TO GOOD EFFECT. THE VERY ABSENCE OF SUCH SEASONINGS, HOWEVER, ALLOWS THE RICH FLAVORS OF THE ONIONS AND LENTILS TO COME THROUGH CLEARLY. SERVE WITH A CLUSTER OF WATERCRESS, A FEW SWEET-AND-SOUR PICKLES, AND A CRUET OF VINEGAR OR KETCHUP.

1 tablespoon butter

1 tablespoon olive oil

2 cups chopped yellow onions

salt and freshly ground pepper

*1 cup green or brown lentils, picked over
    and rinsed*

½ cup finely diced celery

½ cup peeled and finely diced carrot

2 cups fresh bread crumbs

1 egg

vegetable oil for frying

In a skillet over low heat, melt the butter with the oil. Add the onions, cover, and cook over low heat until soft, about 20 minutes. Give them a stir once or twice while they're cooking. Remove the lid and cook, stirring occasionally, until they're browned, meltingly soft, and full of aroma, about 15 minutes. Season well to taste with salt and pepper.

Meanwhile, in a saucepan, combine the lentils, celery, carrot, 1 teaspoon salt, and water to cover by 3 inches. Bring to boil, reduce the heat to medium, and simmer until the lentils are tender, about 30 minutes. Drain well and purée in a food processor, leaving some texture. Transfer to a bowl and stir in the cooked onions and half of the bread crumbs. Season to taste with salt and pepper and stir in the egg. Spread the mixture out on a platter or tray and let it cool so that it will be easier to handle. When cool, form into 3-inch ovals or into rounds 2½ inches across. Spread the remaining bread crumbs on a plate and roll the croquettes in them, coating evenly.

Preheat an oven to 200 degrees F. Pour the oil into a skillet to the depth of ⅛ inch and place over medium-high heat. When hot enough to brown a bread crumb quickly, working in batches, add a layer of the croquettes; do not crowd the pan. Fry until golden brown on all sides, 5 to 8 minutes. Using a slotted spoon, remove them to paper towels to drain, then put in the oven to keep warm while you finish frying the others. Serve hot.

WALNUT AND POTATO CROQUETTES

MAKES 10 TO 12; SERVES 4

N 1913, MRS. WEEDRIDGE FEIRES, THE WIFE OF THE GOVERNOR OF MICHIGAN, WROTE THAT "THESE ARE FINE AND MAKE AN EXCELLENT SUBSTITUTE FOR MEAT." THEY'RE A GOOD MEAT SUBSTITUTE TODAY AS WELL. MRS. FEIRES SUGGESTS SERVING THEM WITH A TOMATO CREAM SAUCE—A KIND OF LADIES' LUNCHEON DISH—OR YOU CAN MAKE DO WITH KETCHUP AND A MOUND OF COLESLAW (PAGE 47) ON THE SIDE. THE POTATO WORKS AS A FILLING BINDER AND THE NUTS ARE WONDERFULLY FULL TASTING. SHE CALLED FOR VIRTUALLY NO SEASONINGS, BUT I'VE TAKEN THE LIBERTY OF BROWNING THE ONIONS AND ADDING SOME SAGE. MAKE THEM SMALL, LIKE THESE, OR HAMBURGER SIZE, AS YOU PREFER.

In a small skillet over medium-high heat, melt the butter. Add the onion and sauté until browned, stirring frequently. Transfer the onion to a bowl and add the walnuts, potatoes, and half of the bread crumbs. Combine well, then mix in the egg, salt, pepper to taste, and the sage.

To form the croquettes, scoop out a heaping tablespoon of the mixture and shape it into an oval. Spread the remaining bread crumbs on a plate and roll the croquettes in them to coat evenly.

Preheat an oven to 200 degrees F. Pour oil into a skillet to a depth of ⅛ inch and place over high heat. Alternatively, melt an equal amount of clarified butter or use a combination of the two. When hot enough to brown a bread crumb quickly, working in batches, add a layer of the croquettes; do not crowd the pan. Fry until golden on all sides, about 5 minutes. Using a slotted spoon, remove them to paper towels to drain, then put in the oven to keep warm while you finish frying the others. Serve hot.

2 tablespoons butter

½ cup grated or finely diced onion

1 cup finely chopped walnuts

1 cup mashed cooked potatoes

2 cups fresh bread crumbs

1 egg

1 teaspoon salt

freshly ground pepper

1 tablespoon chopped sage leaves

vegetable oil and/or clarified butter for frying

chapter four

VEGETABLE

SIDE DISHES

VEGETABLE SIDE DISHES

UNTIL QUITE RECENTLY, AMERICAN COOKBOOKS RELEGATED VEGETABLES TO CHAPTERS TITLED ACCOMPANIMENTS OR SIDE DISHES, CHAPTERS THAT ALSO INCLUDED TWO OTHER IMPORTANT FOODS, BEANS AND GRAINS. It's only recently that books have begun to devote entire chapters to these three foods, even if they're still given a side-dish status.

The slim offerings of older cookbooks suggest that vegetables played a minor part on the American table. Yet, when I've asked people if they ate vegetables when they were growing up, many have replied, "Oh yes, and lots of them!" They then proceeded to reel off the names of the vegetable dishes and to describe how they were cooked and how good they were. Southerners have waxed on about their greens, beans, and hoppin' John. Midwestern farm families have described how corn came at the end of the meal, just before dessert, and how the kids would be sent out to pick it from the patch near the door so it would be really fresh. My New Mexican neighbors still relish walking along the irrigation ditches where they find wild asparagus in the spring and sour chokecherries in the fall.

To be fair, I've also heard numerous lackluster descriptions of quite standard vegetable dishes, from both farm and city people. While families may have differed at their tables, we do know that until modern times vegetables were, for many, a rarity. For lack of quantity alone, they would appear on the side.

Since side dishes do accompany other foods, namely meat, they're often simple and modest, and not meant to be substantial or in any way the center of the plate. With a few changes here and there, they can, however, be transformed so that they fit easily into some other part of the meal—fried okra as an appetizer, or succotash with popovers as a main course. In fact, many of the main-course dishes in this book come from shifting the emphasis and stature of the traditional side dish. Nonetheless, there are still some dishes that do well to remain as straightforward accompaniments to the other foods we eat.

ALABAMA CHRISTMAS LIMAS OR SPECKLED BUTTER BEANS

SERVES 4 TO 6

ONE OF MY FAVORITE COMMUNITY COOKBOOKS, **TREASURED ALABAMA RECIPES,** IS INDEED FILLED WITH TREASURES—MUSCADINE PIE, LOWNDES COUNTY MOLASSES BREAD, A BAKED INDIAN PUDDING WITH GINGER, FIG ICE CREAM, AND A CURSORY MENTION OF BUTTER BEANS COOKED WITH BUTTER, SALT AND PEPPER, "AND A LITTLE OKRA IF YOU LIKE." PERHAPS IT WAS THE STRAIGHTFORWARDNESS OF THE RECIPE THAT MADE IT SOUND SO APPEALING, BUT THESE BEANS ALSO TASTE GOOD. USE DRIED CHRISTMAS LIMAS, AN HEIRLOOM BEAN, OR THE QUICKER-COOKING FROZEN SPECKLED BUTTER BEANS. I DO LIKE THE OKRA, TOO—VERY LITTLE PODS, TRIMMED BUT LEFT WHOLE.

Put the dried limas, water, celery, onion, bay leaves, and the 1 teaspoon butter or oil in a saucepan. Bring to a boil, then lower the heat and simmer, partially covered, until the beans are tender, 1 hour or longer. About halfway through the cooking, when they begin to soften noticeably, add the 1 teaspoon salt.

When the beans are done, fish out the aromatics. Drain off the broth and set it aside. Add the okra, if using, and enough of the reserved broth to make it just a little soupy. Simmer until the okra is tender, about 10 minutes. Taste for salt, season with pepper, and stir in the butter to taste.

VARIATION with frozen butter beans: Cook 3 cups frozen speckled butter beans in water to cover with the aromatics until tender, about 10 minutes. Complete the dish as given, above.

1½ cups dried Christmas lima beans, picked over and rinsed

6 cups water

1 celery stalk, cut into 3 pieces

½ yellow onion stuck with 1 clove

2 small bay leaves

1 teaspoon butter or vegetable oil

1 teaspoon salt, plus salt to taste

freshly ground pepper

1 cup small okra, trimmed but left whole (optional)

butter to taste

CREAMED CABBAGE WITH DILL

SERVES 4 TO 6

INSTEAD OF THE USUAL FLOUR-THICKENED WHITE SAUCE THAT ONCE SMOTHERED NEARLY EVERY AMERICAN HEAD OF CABBAGE, THIS VERSION IS COOKED WITH CREAM, AND IT MAKES A DELECTABLE DISH WITH A THIN BUT HIGHLY AROMATIC SAUCE. YOU CAN EASILY SLIP IN ANOTHER HERB—ROSEMARY GIVES A WINTRY FEEL, AS DO AROMATIC JUNIPER BERRIES. WHEN IT'S AVAILABLE IN THE MARKET, I SOMETIMES ADD SOME GRATED KOHLRABI. SERVE THE CABBAGE AND ITS SAUCE AS A SIDE DISH OR OVER TOASTED RYE BREAD OR EGG NOODLES.

1 head green cabbage, about 2½ pounds

salt

freshly ground pepper

1 cup light cream

2 tablespoons minced dill,
    or 1 tablespoon dill seeds

Core the cabbage and chop the leaves into squares about an inch or so across. Bring a large pot of water to a boil and add salt to taste and the cabbage. Boil, uncovered, for 3 minutes. Drain and rinse with cool water, then press out as much water as you can from the leaves.

About 30 minutes before eating, put the cabbage in a wide skillet with salt and pepper to taste, the cream, and the dill or dill seeds. Bring to a boil, then reduce the heat to low, cover, and stew gently until the cabbage is tender, about 20 minutes. The cream won't be cloying because of the water in the cabbage, but will end up as a thin, flavorful sauce. Serve hot.

PICTURED, TOP TO BOTTOM: CARROTS DELUXE (PAGE 108); CORN, TOMATOES, AND OKRA (PAGE 109); CREAMED CABBAGE WITH DILL (THIS PAGE).

HOMINY SPOON BREAD WITH WHOLE HOMINY

SERVES 4 TO 6

HOMINY IS A STAPLE FOOD OF TWO AREAS, THE DEEP SOUTH AND THE SOUTHWEST, WHERE IT IS CALLED **POSOLE**. IT RECEIVES VERY DIFFERENT TREATMENT IN THESE TWO PLACES WHEN IT COMES TO COOKING, THOUGH. THE HOMINY-BASED DISHES OF THE SOUTH ARE MILD AND SOOTHING, WHETHER MADE OF GRITS OR WHOLE KERNELS OF TREATED CORN, OR BOTH, LIKE THIS ONE. IN THE SOUTHWEST, POSOLE IS COOKED WHOLE AND SERVED IN STEWS MADE HOT WITH RED OR GREEN CHILE. ✸ THIS PUDDING IS FILLED WITH CHEWY NUGGETS OF WHOLE HOMINY. THE CHEESY TANG COMES FROM USING BUTTERMILK RATHER THAN SWEET MILK. QUICK-COOKING GRITS ARE EASY TO FIND AND CAN BE USED, BUT STONE-GROUND GRITS HAVE THE BEST FLAVOR (SEE VARIATION). HOMINY SPOON BREAD CAN BE SERVED ANY TIME OF DAY, YEAR-ROUND, IN A SINGLE LARGE DISH OR INDIVIDUAL CUSTARD CUPS.

---

butter for dish, plus 4 tablespoons butter

4 cups water

2 teaspoons salt

1 cup quick-cooking hominy grits

4 eggs

1½ cups buttermilk

1 can (15 ounces) whole hominy, white or yellow, drained and thoroughly rinsed

freshly ground pepper

Preheat an oven to 400 degrees F. Butter a 2-quart gratin dish.

In a saucepan, bring the water to a boil with the salt and 4 tablespoons butter. Whisk in the grits and cook over medium heat, stirring frequently until thickened, about 4 minutes. Remove from the heat and set aside.

Beat the eggs well, then stir in the buttermilk. Beat this mixture into the grits, then add the whole hominy. Season to taste with pepper.

Pour the mixture into the prepared baking dish. Bake until puffed and browned on top, about 1 hour. Let cool for 5 minutes, then serve.

VARIATION with stone-ground hominy grits: Bring the water to a boil in the top pan of a double boiler, add the salt, and whisk in the grits. Stir until the texture is thick and even, after a few minutes, then set the pan over boiling water, cover, and cook for 40 minutes. Complete the dish as given above.

FRIED BLUE CORN MUSH WITH GREEN CHILE

MAKES 12 TO 15 SLICES; SERVES 6

THIS RECALLS THE CORN MUSH OF THE EASTERN AND PLAINS STATES AS WELL AS ITALIAN POLENTA, BUT HERE THE CORN IS THE TRADITIONAL HOPI BLUE CORN. I HAVE ENJOYED THIS DISH MANY TIMES AT THE HOPI CULTURAL CENTER IN ARIZONA, IN VIEW OF THE DISTANT SAN FRANCISCO PEAKS WHERE THE KACHINAS DWELL. I COOK THE MUSH IN A DOUBLE BOILER WHILE I ROAST THE CHILES. THAT WAY IT COOKS WELL AND WITHOUT MY ATTENTION. SINCE CORNMEAL MUSH HAS TO BE VERY FIRM BEFORE FRYING (IT REALLY IS A WAY OF USING LEFTOVER CEREAL), PLAN TO MAKE IT A FEW HOURS AHEAD OF TIME, OR EVEN THE DAY BEFORE. SERVE WITH FRIED EGGS AND THE RED CHILE SAUCE ON PAGE 89.

Make a slurry in a bowl by stirring 1 cup of the water into the cornmeal. Put the rest of the water in the top pan of a double boiler and bring it to a boil directly over the heat. Whisk in the slurry, add the salt and sage, and stir until it the mixture has begun to thicken, after a few minutes. Set the pan over boiling water, cover, and let cook until very thick, about 30 minutes.

Meanwhile, roast the chiles directly over a flame or under a preheated broiler until the skins are evenly blistered all over. Put them in a bowl, cover with a plate, and set aside to steam for 15 minutes. Remove the skins with your fingers and pull out the stems and seeds. Chop the chiles and stir them into the cornmeal.

When the cornmeal is finished cooking, turn it into a bread pan, smooth the top, and cover with waxed paper. Refrigerate until it has cooled and hardened, after a few hours.

Turn the firm cornmeal out of the pan, and cut into slices about ½ inch thick. Dredge them in the flour or cornmeal. Pour oil into 1 or 2 heavy skillets to a depth of ⅛ inch and place over medium-high heat. When the oil is hot, add several pieces of the cornmeal and fry until browned and crisp, about 4 minutes on each side. If using 1 pan, keep the finished pieces in a warm oven (200 degrees F) until all are done. Serve hot.

4 cups water

1⅓ cups blue cornmeal, or yellow if blue is unavailable

1 teaspoon salt

½ teaspoon crumbled dried sage

2 long, green New Mexican chiles

all-purpose flour or blue cornmeal

sunflower seed oil for frying

PECAN-COVERED GRIT BALLS

MAKES 16 LARGE OR 32 SMALL; SERVES 4 TO 6

THE BRONXVILLE WOMEN'S CLUB COOKBOOK IS PREFACED BY THE STATEMENT THAT THIS COLLECTION OF FAVORITE RECIPES BY CLUB MEMBERS IS "VISIBLE PROOF THAT THEY ARE HOMEMAKERS," WITH A CAPITAL H. THE BOOK IS FILLED WITH SOLID EVIDENCE TO BACK UP THAT ASSERTION—A YELLOW TOMATO MARMALADE, SPICED PEACHES MADE FROM DRIED FRUIT, AND A CHEESE SOUFFLÉ SERVED WITH A MEXICAN SAUCE CONSISTING OF KETCHUP AND GREEN PEPPERS—UNDOUBTEDLY QUITE ADVENTUROUS FOR THE TIME. ❀ GRIT BALLS (IN ANOTHER BOOK, THE NAME IS SCOFFED AT!) CONSIST OF PLAIN GRITS, SHAPED INTO BALLS, COATED IN EGG, DUSTED IN PECANS, AND FRIED. THEY'RE CRISP, CRUNCHY, AND GOLDEN BROWN ON THE OUTSIDE, PLAIN AND SOFT INSIDE. YOU CAN POUR MAPLE SYRUP ON THEM OR SERVE THEM WITH GREENS. OR YOU MIGHT EMBELLISH THE ORIGINAL BY LACING THE GRITS WITH SLICED GREEN ONIONS AND A CUP OF GRATED CHEDDAR CHEESE. HAVING NO CLUE AS TO THE TRADITIONAL BRONXVILLE SIZE, I MADE MINE LARGE, BUT I SUSPECT THEY'RE MORE LIKE HUSH PUPPIES, ABOUT THE SIZE OF LARGE MARBLES. INSTANT GRITS THAT COOK IN ABOUT 7 MINUTES ARE USED HERE BECAUSE THEY'RE EASY TO FIND, BUT I PREFER THE STONE-GROUND VARIETY, WHICH TAKES ABOUT 40 MINUTES. USE A DOUBLE BOILER AND SAVE THE STIRRING.

In a saucepan, bring the water to a boil. Add 1 teaspoon of the salt and gradually stir in the grits. Cover and cook, stirring occasionally, until nice and thick, 5 to 7 minutes. When done, pour them into a pan and set aside to cool. (This can be done well ahead of time.) When cool, dip your hands into cold water, pick up some of the grits, and roll them into balls, large like golf balls or small like marbles, as you like. Set them on waxed paper as you work.

Beat the egg in a pie plate. In a second pie plate, combine the bread crumbs and pecans and season them with the remaining ½ teaspoon salt and a few gridings of pepper. With one hand, dip each ball into the egg, then drop it into the crumbs. With the other hand, roll it around so that it is coated.

In a wide skillet, melt the butter with the oil over medium-high heat. When hot enough to sizzle a bread crumb, fry the balls until they're golden all over, turning them as they cook. This will take only a few minutes. You'll need to do this in 2 batches, or use 2 pans. Set them briefly on paper towels to drain, then transfer to a plate and serve hot.

3 cups water

1½ teaspoons salt

¾ cup quick-cooking grits

1 egg

1 cup fresh bread crumbs

1 cup finely chopped pecans

freshly ground pepper

2 tablespoons butter

½ cup vegetable oil

CARROTS DELUXE

SERVES 4

THESE MODEST GARNISHES MIGHT NOT SEEM SO DELUXE TO US TODAY—IN FACT, **DELUXE** IS A WORD THAT'S HARDLY EVER USED ANYMORE, EXCEPT FOR CRUISES OR TO DESCRIBE A PARTICULARLY CLASSY MODEL OF SOMETHING. BUT WHAT DOES MAKE THIS CARROT DISH TRULY DELUXE IS THE INGREDIENTS: START WITH SWEET CARROTS, FRESH SHALLOTS, AND GLOSSY PARSLEY LEAVES—ALL FOUND IN A FARMERS' MARKET. SIMPLE ENOUGH INGREDIENTS, BUT ESSENTIAL AND GOOD. USE ENOUGH SHALLOT AND PARSLEY SO THAT CARROTS ARE COATED WITH THEM. THE VARIETY AND SIZE OF THE CARROT DETERMINE HOW IT'S CUT: LEFT WHOLE, DIVIDED INTO HALVES OR QUARTERED LENGTHWISE, OR SLICED INTO BATONS OR ROUNDS.

1 pound carrots
¼ cup finely diced shallots
¼ cup chopped parsley
1 or 2 tablespoons butter
salt and freshly ground pepper

Peel the carrots, then cut them into whatever size is appropriate for the shape and size of the carrot (see note). Steam them over boiling water until they're tender, but not mushy, 5 to 8 minutes, depending on how the carrots were cut.

Set a sauté pan over high heat with the shallots, parsley, and butter. Add the steamed carrots and sauté, shaking the pan back and forth, until the carrots are coated and the shallots have just begun to gain a little color, after 4 or 5 minutes. Season to taste with salt and pepper and serve.

CORN, TOMATOES, AND OKRA

SERVES 4 TO 8

MANY VERSIONS OF THIS SIMPLE GUMBO ARE FOUND THROUGHOUT THE SOUTHERN STATES. THE CORN HELPS MITIGATE THE OKRA'S DUBIOUS TEXTURE, WHICH IS WHAT BINDS THIS DISH INTO A STEW. IF IT ISN'T FOR YOU, LEAVE THE PODS WHOLE, CAREFULLY TRIMMED OF THEIR STEMS, BUT NOT CUT INTO AT ALL. SERVE OVER A PLATE OF CAROLINA LONG-GRAIN RICE TO DRINK UP THE JUICES. TO BE GOOD, OKRA SHOULD BE VERY SMALL, THE PODS NO LONGER THAN 3 INCHES AND PREFERABLY ONLY 2. THEY GO QUICKLY FROM TENDER TO TOUGH AS THEY INCREASE IN SIZE.

In a skillet over medium heat, warm the butter or butter and oil. Add the onion, bay leaves, thyme, basil, and red pepper flakes and sauté, stirring frequently, until limp, about 5 minutes. Add the bell pepper and cook until softened, then add the tomatoes, okra, and water. Simmer, uncovered, for 15 minutes, then add the corn and cook until the corn is heated through and tender, 3 to 4 minutes. Season to taste with salt and pepper. Serve hot.

3 tablespoons butter, or 1½ tablespoons
each butter and canola oil
1 small yellow onion, finely diced
2 bay leaves
½ teaspoon dried thyme
½ teaspoon dried basil
½ teaspoon red pepper flakes
1 green bell pepper, seeded and finely
diced
3 large, ripe tomatoes, peeled, seeded, and
chopped
2 cups small okra, left whole or sliced
into ¼-inch-thick rounds
½ cup water
kernels from 3 ears of corn
(about 2 cups)
salt and freshly ground pepper

BROILED EGGPLANT ROUNDS WITH TOMATOES AND CHEESE

MAKES 12 ROUNDS; SERVES 4

THE INSPIRATION FOR THESE EGGPLANT ROUNDS COMES FROM AN IDAHO COMMUNITY COOKBOOK, ALTHOUGH VERSIONS ARE REPEATED IN SIMILAR BOOKS FROM THE MIDWEST. THE ORIGINAL CALLS FOR THAT UBIQUITOUS COMBINATION OF "AMERICAN CHEESE" AND CRACKER CRUMBS, A COATING APPLIED TO AN ALARMINGLY GOOD MANY OF OUR VEGETABLES. BUT THIS DISH CAN BE QUITE CHOICE IF YOU WORK FROM THE BEST OF THE SEASON—FIRM EGGPLANTS WITH NO SEEDS, ONE OF THE LITTLE, SWEET HEIRLOOM TOMATO VARIETIES NOW BEING GROWN—AND ANY OF OUR GOOD CHEESES—TELEME, CHEDDAR, FRESH GOAT, JACK (I'VE TRIED THEM ALL)—PLUS FRESH BREAD CRUMBS. SERVE THESE LITTLE MOUTHFULS AS AN APPETIZER, A LIGHT LUNCHEON DISH, OR A SIDE DISH.

2 very fresh slender eggplants,
    about 2½ inches in diameter
    and 8 inches long
4 tomatoes, about the same diameter
    as the eggplants
safflower oil or olive oil for frying
salt and freshly ground pepper
12 thin slices cheese, about the
    size of the eggplant rounds,
    or ¼ cup crumbled goat cheese
4 tablespoons fresh bread crumbs,
    tossed in olive oil or melted
    butter to moisten

Trim the eggplants and tomatoes and slice into rounds a little less than ½ inch thick. You should have 12 slices of each. Heat enough oil in a heavy skillet to cover the bottom generously. When it is almost smoking, add the eggplant rounds just to cover the pan without crowding (you may need to work in 2 batches). Quickly turn them over so that both sides are lightly coated in oil, then cook over medium-high heat until browned on the first side. Turn and cook until browned on the second side, about 10 minutes in all. Set them on paper towels to drain briefly, then transfer them to a baking sheet.

Lightly season the eggplant with salt and pepper. Cover each round with a piece of cheese (or about 1 teaspoon of goat cheese) and top with a tomato slice. Season again, then cover with the bread crumbs. (Minus adding the bread crumbs, the eggplant can be prepared up to this point, several hours in advance and held in the refrigerator.)

Preheat the broiler and broil about 5 inches under the heat until the crumbs are browned, about 3 minutes. Serve hot.

FRIED OKRA

SERVES 8

THIS IS PROBABLY THE ONLY WAY MOST NON-SOUTHERNERS WILL EAT OKRA SINCE IT ENDS UP NICE AND CRISP. NO ONE FEELS THEY SHOULD EAT FRIED FOODS MUCH, BUT FRIED OKRA IS ONE OF THOSE GOOD ONES, ESPECIALLY IF YOU ARE FROM THE SOUTH AND MISS THIS KIND OF THING. IT IS, IN FACT, THE FIRST THING MY ARKANSAN HUSBAND COOKED FOR ME. JUST SERVE IT AS AN APPETIZER, ALONG WITH SOME FRESH THINGS, SO THAT A LITTLE GOES A LONG WAY. THIS RECIPE MAKES EIGHT SMALL SERVINGS.

1 pound small okra

all-purpose flour

1 egg, beaten

1 tablespoon water

about 1 cup fine-ground cornmeal, dried bread crumbs, or cracker crumbs

freshly ground pepper

vegetable oil for frying

½ teaspoon salt

The okra has to be small, fresh, and tender—3 inches at the most. Cut off the stem ends and the tips, then slice into rounds about ⅓ inch thick.

Put the flour in a shallow bowl or pie plate. In another bowl, beat the egg with the water. In a third bowl, combine the cornmeal or crumbs and pepper to taste. Toss the okra in the flour, then dip them into the egg, followed by the cornmeal or cracker crumbs. Set them on a plate.

Pour the oil into a heavy cast-iron skillet to a depth of 2 inches and heat over medium-high heat. When hot enough to sizzle a bread crumb, add the okra, in small batches, and fry until golden, about 3 minutes. Set on a paper towel to drain briefly, then transfer to a serving basket or platter when all are done. Sprinkle with salt and serve immediately.

MENNONITE PEAS

SERVES 4

TWO HUNDRED YEARS AGO, IN HER BOOK **AMERICAN COOKERY**, AMELIA SIMMONS MADE REFERENCE TO SEVEN VARIETIES OF PEAS. THEY MUST HAVE BEEN TOUGH, FOR EARLY RECIPES ASK US TO COOK THEM FOR AT LEAST AN HOUR. BUT IF PEAS ARE TENDER AND COOKED BUT BRIEFLY, THIS DISH, WHOSE CLASSIC SIMPLICITY CARRIES IT BEYOND THE MENNONITE COMMUNITY, IS ONE OF THE BEST. THE RECIPE, FROM **FOODS OF OUR FATHERS** (PUBLISHED IN 1941), CALLED FOR BIG BUT TENDER ENGLISH PEAS. TODAY THE POPULAR EDIBLE-POD PEA IS A GOOD ONE TO USE AS WELL. I SOMETIMES USE A MIXTURE OF ENGLISH PEAS AND EDIBLE-POD PEAS, SUCH AS SNOW PEAS—WHATEVER LOOKS BEST FROM THE MARKET OR GARDEN. ALTHOUGH THEY'RE NOT CALLED FOR, SOME MINCED SHALLOT AND SOME TENDER MINT OR BASIL LEAVES, THINLY SLICED, ARE CERTAINLY GOOD HERE TOO, ADDED WITH THE BUTTER.

If using pod peas, shuck them. If using edible-pod peas, remove the flower end and strings, if any, but don't shuck them. Bring a pot of water to a boil, add salt to taste, and throw in the peas. Boil until they're tender and bright green, 2 to 3 minutes, then pour into a colander and shake off as much water as possible. Put them in a bowl, towel off any extra water, then toss with salt, if needed, white pepper and butter to taste.

*1 pound English pod peas,
    or edible-pod peas*
salt
freshly ground white pepper
unsalted butter

POTATOES

WE HAVE LONG THOUGHT OF POTATOES AS CHEAP AND ALWAYS AVAILABLE, SO IT IS HARD TO IMAGINE THAT THIS WASN'T ALWAYS SO. Even in Idaho there was a time when it was necessary to stretch Sunday's potatoes to make them go further. In American cookbooks, there are more recipes for potatoes than any other vegetable. *The New Settlement Cookbook* from 1945 gives potatoes their own chapter, as does James Beard many years later. Baked potatoes, even stuffed ones, were mentioned as a favorite dish in a 1934 cookbook from Brownsville, North Carolina, and mashed potatoes in one form or another are still a favorite.

BAKED STUFFED POTATOES

DARK BROWN IDAHO BAKERS OR PEBBLY FLESHED RUSSETS ARE THE POTATOES FOR BAKING. DON'T WRAP THEM IN FOIL; THEY'LL ONLY STEAM AND ONE USUALLY WANTS THE SKIN CRISP. Look for potatoes that are organically grown so that you can eat the skin. Scrub them well, then bake at 375 degrees F until they feel soft when you squeeze them, about an hour. Make a big X on the top with a knife, then push the ends toward the middle to force up the steaming flesh. Do this right away so that the potatoes don't become sodden. Add what you will—butter or olive oil, salt and freshly ground pepper, snipped chives, chopped herbs, grated cheese, or the Dutch Cheese Sandwich Filling on page 59.

IRISH POTATOES

SERVES 4

ITHINK LOTS OF PEOPLE HAVE HAD SOME DISH IN THEIR BACKGROUND CALLED IRISH POTATOES. COMMONLY, IT IS LEFTOVER BOILED POTATOES FRIED WITH GREEN PEPPERS AND ONIONS OR SOME OTHER VERSION OF THE FAMOUS POTATOES O'BRIEN FROM JACK'S RESTAURANT IN NEW YORK. THEY ARE GREAT ANY TIME OF DAY FROM BREAKFAST TO A LATE-NIGHT SUPPER, AND ALMOST BEG FOR A FRIED OR POACHED EGG PERCHED ON TOP. THESE WOULD HAVE BEEN MADE WITH ALL BUTTER (OR BACON DRIPPINGS) AND PLENTY OF IT. THIS VERSION IS MORE MODEST FOR OUR TIMES.

Put the potatoes in a saucepan with water to cover and bring to a boil. Cook until tender when pierced with a knife but not falling apart, 15 to 20 minutes. Drain and let cool, then peel and slice thinly.

Heat 4 teaspoons each of the butter and oil in a very wide skillet over medium-high heat. Add the potatoes and fry, stirring occasionally, until nicely browned on both sides, about 25 minutes in all. The browning is important to their success—it's the best part. Season the potatoes well with salt and pepper while they cook.

Meanwhile, in a second, smaller pan, heat the remaining butter and oil over high heat, add the onion and sauté until golden and crisp around the edges, about 10 minutes. Season with salt. Add the bell pepper to the onion, sauté for 1 or 2 minutes, and then add the whole mixture to the potatoes. Gently combine them with a soft rubber scraper so that they don't mush up. Pile them onto a platter, add the parsley, and serve.

1½ pounds white or red boiling potatoes

2 tablespoons butter

2 tablespoons safflower oil or sunflower oil

salt and freshly ground pepper

1 large white or yellow onion, cut into 1-inch squares

1 green bell pepper, seeded and finely diced

chopped parsley

MASHED POTATOES WITH CARROTS

SERVES 6

A PRETTY, ORANGE-FLECKED PURÉE, THIS RECIPE HAS BEEN POPULAR WITH A DANISH-AMERICAN FAMILY FOR OVER A CENTURY. THE TELLER'S GRANDMOTHER CALLED IT "STUMP."

Steam the potatoes in their jackets until very tender, about 20 minutes. Remove them then steam the carrots until they're tender, about 15 minutes.

Grasp the hot potatoes in a towel and slip off their skins. Put them in a bowl with the carrots and mash to a purée, adding enough milk, light cream, or even the cooking liquid to lighten the mixture. Stir in butter to taste, season with salt and pepper, and stir in all but a teaspoon or so of the parsley or dill. Smooth the purée into a dish and sprinkle the rest of the chopped herb on top.

1 pound small, red boiling potatoes
½ pound carrots, peeled and cut into
  2-inch chunks
milk, light cream, or cooking water
butter
salt and freshly ground pepper
2 tablespoons chopped parsley or dill

CARAMELIZED FRIED GREEN TOMATOES

SERVES 4

WHEREVER THERE ARE GREEN TOMATOES, AND THAT'S ALMOST EVERYWHERE AND NOT JUST THE SOUTH, THERE'S A WAY TO FRY THEM. THEY'RE ALWAYS COATED AND USUALLY IN CORNMEAL. COMMONLY THEY ARE SEASONED WITH SALT AND PEPPER, OTHER TIMES WITH SPICES AND PARMESAN CHEESE, AND STILL OTHER TIMES WITH BROWN SUGAR AND EVEN—IN THE MOST LUXURIOUS VERSION I FOUND—FINISHED WITH CREAM. THIS VERSION HAS A BROWN-SUGAR GLAZE, WHICH MAKES THE TOMATOES SWEET-TART, A RATHER PLEASANT CHANGE FROM THE USUAL.

4 large, green tomatoes

1 cup yellow cornmeal

1½ teaspoons salt

2 teaspoons freshly ground pepper

safflower oil for frying

a few tablespoons light or dark brown sugar

Slice the stem ends off the tomatoes, then slice them into rounds about ½ inch thick. Mix the cornmeal, salt, and pepper in a pie plate, then firmly press the tomatoes into the mixture so that it sticks, coating both sides.

Film a heavy, wide skillet with oil and set it over medium heat. When the oil is hot, add the tomatoes and fry until browned on the bottom, about 5 minutes. Turn them over and sprinkle brown sugar over the tops. When the second side is browned, carefully turn the tomatoes over so that the sugared side is face down. Let them cook for about 1 minute and, while they are cooking, sprinkle a little sugar over what are now the tops. Flip them over one more time and cook the second sides just long enough to caramelize the sugar, about 1 minute more. Serve hot.

SWEET POTATO PURÉE WITH BLACK WALNUTS

SERVES 6 TO 8

IN THIS ILLINOIS RECIPE, A SWEET POTATO PURÉE WAS PERCHED ON RINGS OF CANNED PINEAPPLE (FINE AS LONG AS YOU DON'T ADD MARSHMALLOWS, TOO!). ACTUALLY, THE MILD ACIDITY OF PINEAPPLE IS GOOD WITH SWEET POTATOES — BUT THE DISH IS BETTER IF THE PINEAPPLE IS BROKEN UP AND STIRRED INTO THE PURÉE. IF USING PINEAPPLE DOESN'T APPEAL TO YOU, ADD A FEW TABLESPOONS OF MOLASSES — ANOTHER EXCELLENT ACCOMPANIMENT. SO IS BOURBON. BLACK WALNUTS, A SENSATIONAL ADDITION TO NEARLY ANYTHING, ARE THE CROWNING TOUCH, MAKING THIS A WORTHY DISH FOR THE HOLIDAY TABLE. PECANS CAN TAKE THEIR PLACE IF BLACK WALNUTS AREN'T AVAILABLE.

Peel the yams and cut them into chunks. Steam until completely soft when pierced with a knife, 15 to 20 minutes.

Remove the yams to a bowl and mash with a potato masher or a wooden spoon, adding as much butter as you allow, until you have a fairly smooth mixture. Season to taste with salt, pepper, and ginger, and then stir in the pineapple and the nuts. Serve right away.

Or, if you prefer to serve them later, preheat an oven to 375 degrees F. Omit the nuts, smooth the purée into a buttered baking dish, and bake until heated through, about 25 minutes, stirring in the nuts during the last 10 minutes.

2 pounds yams, preferably Garnet
or Jewel
butter
salt and freshly ground pepper
½ teaspoon ground ginger, or more
to taste
½ cup chopped pineapple, preferably fresh
½ cup black walnut pieces, plus more
for sprinkling on top

POTATO LATKES

SERVES 4 TO 6

ACONTRIBUTION FROM EASTERN EUROPE AND FROM JEWISH IMMIGRANTS IN PARTICULAR, THESE CAKES ARE A TRADITIONAL PART OF CHANUKAH, BUT ARE A FAVORITE OF NEARLY EVERYONE EVERY TIME THEY'RE MADE. SERVE THEM WITH SOUR CREAM AND APPLESAUCE, OR WITH SOUR CREAM AND SNIPPED CHIVES. EXACTLY HOW THEY ARE MADE (ARE THE POTATOES RINSED OR NOT?) AND HOW LARGE THEY ARE (TWO-BITE SIZE OR BIGGER) ARE, AS WITH MANY TRADITIONAL DISHES, ALWAYS SUBJECT TO DEBATE. IT COMES DOWN IN THE END TO PERSONAL PREFERENCE, OR TO WHAT YOUR MOTHER DID. IT IS UNDEBATABLE, THOUGH, THAT LATKES TASTE BEST AS SOON AS THEY'RE MADE, SO PLAN TO COOK THEM TO ORDER.

5 large russet potatoes, about 2½ pounds total

1 large yellow onion

3 eggs

¼ cup all-purpose flour, or more as needed

2 to 3 teaspoons salt (potatoes need a lot)

freshly ground pepper

vegetable oil for frying

Applesauce (page 19) and sour cream for serving

Peel the potatoes and grate them on the large holes of a hand-held grater. Transfer them to a sieve set over a bowl and, using your hands or the back of a wooden spoon, press out as much moisture as you can. Starch will collect under the potato water. Some cooks pour off the water and add the starch back to the potatoes, as a binder. Grate the onion on the same grater and combine it with the potato in a clean bowl. Add the potato starch, if you like.

Beat the eggs in a small bowl. Add them to the potatoes, then stir in enough flour to make a light batter. Add the salt and the pepper to taste. Fry a nugget of the potato mixture, then taste it to make sure there's enough salt.

In a large, heavy skillet over medium-high heat, warm enough oil to come ⅛ to ¼ inch up the sides of the pan. It should be good and hot but not smoking. Drop the batter by tablespoonfuls or ¼ cupfuls into the hot oil. Gently press on them to flatten them out. Don't crowd the pan or the latkes will become soggy. Fry until golden on the bottom, about 3 minutes, then turn and brown the second side. Remove to paper towels to drain briefly, then serve as soon as you can, with the Applesauce and sour cream.

BEETS WITH APPLES AND ONIONS

SERVES 4

THE PRACTICE OF COOKING VEGETABLES WITH ONIONS AND APPLES OCCURS IN MORE THAN A FEW AMERICAN RECIPES. INITIALLY, I WAS A BIT RESISTANT TO THEIR PAIRING WITH BEETS, BUT NOW I CAN SAY THAT IT IS A STRIKINGLY INTERESTING AND BOLD COMBINATION. INDEED, IT IS A DISH THAT'S PRACTICALLY INHALED AT OUR HOUSE. WHILE YOU CAN SERVE IT AS A SIDE DISH, LEFTOVERS MAKE A GREAT LITTLE SALAD OR ITEM ON A COMPOSED-SALAD PLATE.

4 beets

2 Granny Smith or other tart green
    apples

½ onion, diced

1 teaspoon salt

2 tablespoons fresh lemon juice

⅛ teaspoon freshly grated nutmeg

1 tablespoon brown sugar (optional)

about 1½ tablespoons butter

Steam the beets over boiling water until tender-firm when pierced with the tip of a knife, 30 to 45 minutes depending on their size. When they're cool enough to handle, peel, then dice into ½-inch cubes. Place in a bowl.

Preheat an oven to 350 degrees F. Lightly butter a 1-quart baking dish. Core the apples but do not peel. Cut into small cubes; you should have about 2 cups. Add to the bowl along with the onion, salt, lemon juice, and nutmeg. If you favor extra sweetness, add the sugar. Toss well.

Place the vegetables in the prepared baking dish and dot the top with the butter. Cover and bake until the apples are tender and the flavors have melded, about 1 hour. Serve right from the oven, warm, or even chilled.

SUCCOTASH OR MI'I SIC QUOTASH

SERVES 4

ATRUE NATIVE AMERICAN DISH, **MI'I SIC QUOTASH**—OR SUCCOTASH, AS IT IS MORE COMMONLY KNOWN— IS A WONDERFUL, SOUL-SATISFYING FOOD THAT HAS BEEN DONE A GREAT DISSERVICE BY THE FROZEN VERSION. IN **NEWINGTON'S BICENTENNIAL COOKBOOK**, A CONTRIBUTOR WRITES THAT "MANY PEOPLE DO NOT KNOW HOW TO MAKE A GOOD SUCCOTASH, BUT ALL OF OUR FAMILY HAS HAD PRAISE ON OUR GRANDMOTHER'S WAY OF MAKING IT." HER METHOD WAS TO BOIL LIMA OR CRANBERRY BEANS UNTIL DONE, ADD FRESH-CUT CORN—JUST THE TOPS OF THE KERNELS—AND THEN THE SCRAPINGS. "DO NOT STIR OR BOIL," MRS. SWEETON WARNS. "IT IS THE SCRAPINGS THAT MAKE THE DIFFERENCE BETWEEN CORN AND BEANS AND SUCCOTASH—MORE SCRAPINGS AND NO STIRRING." TO MAKE THIS SIDE DISH INTO A MAIN DISH, SERVE IT OVER A MOUND OF CHEESE GRITS, SPOON IT OVER BISCUITS, OR TUCK IT INTO POPOVERS. SUCCOTASH CAN ALSO ABSORB OTHER SUMMER VEGETABLES, LIKE TOMATOES, PEPPERS, AND SQUASHES, AND CAN BE BUILT INTO A GREAT HARVEST STEW.

Shuck the corn and pull off the silks. Using a sharp knife, slice off the tops of the kernels and put them in a bowl. Turn the knife over and, using the dull side, press it down the length of the cobs, squeezing out the rest of the corn and the milk into another bowl. These are the scrapings.

For shell beans, put the beans in a saucepan with water to cover. Bring to a boil and cook until tender, 25 to 40 minutes. For frozen limas, cook for 5 minutes in 4 tablespoons of boiling water. When done, transfer the beans to a 10-inch skillet along with the corn kernels, butter, and enough of the cooking water just to cover. Bring to a boil, then reduce the heat to low and simmer uncovered for 5 minutes. Stir in the corn scrapings and continue to cook gently, without stirring, for 10 minutes. The water will have mostly cooked off, leaving the sweet corn and beans bound with the corn milk. Season to taste with salt and pepper. Serve hot.

4 ears of yellow corn, fresh from the garden
1 cup fresh or frozen lima beans or shell beans
2 tablespoons butter
salt and freshly ground pepper

chapter five

A FEW

DESSERTS

A FEW DESSERTS

THE SETTLERS OF THIS COUNTRY MAY HAVE STRUGGLED WITH VEGETABLES, BUT THEY WERE GOOD BAKERS AND FOND OF DESSERTS. Not only are there a great many recipes for desserts, but sweet things appear early on in the tables of contents of many cookbooks, instead of at the end, where they've been residing now for quite a few years, in harmony with the flow of the meal. As recently as our bicentennial year, one cookbook I found started with appetizers, breads and muffins, and then, not atypically, leapt right into puddings, pies, cookies and bars, frostings, fillings, and ice creams. Savory foods followed. At least six or seven chapters in the big compendium cookbooks are devoted to desserts; fewer, of course, appear in smaller books.

A good many of our traditional desserts are fruit based, and some of them—namely pies, crisps, and cobblers—have served farm families for breakfast as well as for supper. (My partially midwestern background definitely approves of pie for breakfast.) These few desserts feature our undying love for the apple, our native grape, buckles and grunts, southern figs, and a plate of American cheeses. It was hard to choose—there are so many and they're so good!

BLUEBERRY COBBLER

SERVES 6 TO 8

BUCKLES AND COBBLERS REFER TO FRUITS BAKED UNDER A BISCUIT COVERING. IT'S THE DOUGH, SPOONED CLOSELY OVER THE TOP, THAT BAKES TO A COBBLED OR BUCKLED APPEARANCE, GIVING THE DISH THE LOOK THAT THE NAME SUGGESTS. BLUEBERRIES, UNLESS THEY'RE PICKED IN THE WILD, NEED MORE THAN WHITE SUGAR FOR SEASONING TO MAKE UP FOR THEIR SOMETIMES WATERY FLAVOR. MOLASSES IMPARTS TO FRUITS JUST THE DEPTH THEY WANT, YET THEY DON'T TASTE LIKE MOLASSES. SERVE WARM WITH A PITCHER OF COLD CREAM OR VANILLA ICE CREAM.

Preheat an oven to 350 degrees F.

To make the filling pick over the blueberries and remove any stems or bruised fruits, then rinse well. Stir together the sugar, cinnamon, nutmeg, and cloves in a bowl. Put the berries in a 2-quart gratin dish, sprinkle all but 1½ tablespoons of the sugar mixture over them, and then drizzle over the molasses and lemon or lime juice. Stir gently with a rubber scraper, then shake the dish to even the fruit. Put the gratin dish in the oven for 5 minutes to release some of the berries' juices. Remove from the oven and raise the heat to 425 degrees F.

To make the topping, combine the flour, salt, and baking powder in a bowl. Using 2 knives or your fingers, cut in the butter until the mixture forms coarse, uneven crumbs. In a separate bowl, beat the egg with the milk or cream. Stir it into the flour mixture with a few swift strokes. Spoon the dough in small, even spoonfuls over the berries. Sprinkle the top with the reserved 1½ tablespoons sugar mixture.

Set the dish on a baking sheet and bake on a rack in the center of the oven until bubbling and the topping is browned, about 30 minutes. Remove and let cool for at least 15 minutes before serving. Serve warm.

Fruit filling

4 cups blueberries

6 tablespoons sugar

½ teaspoon ground cinnamon

½ teaspoon freshly grated nutmeg

⅛ teaspoon ground cloves

¼ cup molasses

2 tablespoons fresh lemon or lime juice

Topping

1¾ cups all-purpose flour

¼ teaspoon salt

2½ teaspoons baking powder

7 tablespoons chilled butter, cut into
*   small pieces*

1 egg

½ cup plus 1 tablespoon milk or
*   light cream*

SUMMER TREAT FIG ICE CREAM

MAKES ABOUT 6 CUPS; SERVES 8

ALMOST EVERY OLD COLLECTION OF SOUTHERN RECIPES I LOOKED AT HAD FIG DESSERTS, OF WHICH THIS IS ONE. YOU'LL WANT DEAD-RIPE, JUICY FIGS. THE ICE CREAM HAS NO EXTRA FLAVORINGS, BUT I ALWAYS FIND THAT A LITTLE CLOVE AND LEMON BRING OUT THIS FRUIT'S FLAVOR. YOU MAY WISH TO ADD THEM, TOO. IF THE FIGS ARE STILL A LITTLE GREEN AND NOT QUITE UP TO PAR, CHOP THEM UP AND COOK THEM FIRST WITH 1 CUP OF THE SUGAR OR ¾ CUP LIGHT HONEY, THEN PROCEED WITH THE RECIPE.

2 pints ripe, sweet figs (about 1 pound or a little more)

1 quart half-and-half, or 2 cups each milk and heavy cream

1½ cups sugar

6 eggs, separated, or 3 egg yolks and 6 whites

pinch of salt

¼ teaspoon ground cloves

finely grated zest of 1 lemon

Rinse the figs, for they're usually dusty. If the skins are thick, peel them. If they're thin, you can leave them on. In any case, chop them roughly, then place in a bowl and mash them with a fork into a thick, chunky purée.

Pour the half-and-half or milk and cream in a saucepan and add 1 cup of the sugar. Place over medium heat and heat just to boiling, stirring to dissolve the sugar. Remove from the heat. Gradually whisk the hot cream into a bowl containing the egg yolks. Add the salt, cloves, lemon zest, and figs and refrigerate until well chilled.

When the fig mixture is cold, whip the egg whites in a spacious bowl until they form soft peaks. Gradually add the remaining sugar and continue to beat until a soft meringue is formed. Fold the meringue into the figs, then freeze in an ice cream maker according to the manufacturer's instructions, or in a large tray in the freezer.

CONCORD GRAPE PIE

MAKES ONE 9-INCH DOUBLE-CRUST PIE; SERVES 6 TO 8

THIS PIE IS TRULY AMERICA'S OWN, MADE FROM OUR NATIVE CONCORDS IN THE NORTHEAST AND MIDWEST, OR MUSCADINES IN THE SOUTH. THEIR FLAVOR IS RICH, LIKE BLACKBERRIES, AND I BELIEVE THIS IS THE BEST PIE THERE IS. I FIND THE SMALLER GRAPES THAT I BUY FROM LOCAL FARMERS TO BE BETTER SUITED TO PIES THAN COMMERCIAL GRAPES, WHICH ARE SOMETIMES TOO WATERY. THIS IS AN INTERESTING PIE TO SERVE WITH CHEESE AS LONG AS IT IS NOT PIPING HOT, AND IT SHOULDN'T BE, IN ANY CASE. TRY SLICES OF MONTEREY JACK, TELEME, A MILD GOAT CHEESE, OR CHEDDAR.

Pie crust
2½ cups all-purpose flour
½ teaspoon salt
12 tablespoons (¾ cup) unsalted chilled
    butter, cut into small pieces
6 to 7 tablespoons ice water

Filling
2½ pounds purple or white Concord
    grapes
½ to ¾ cup sugar
4 to 6 tablespoons all-purpose flour, or
    1 tablespoon quick-cooking tapioca
grated zest of 1 lemon
1 to 2 tablespoons fresh lemon juice, to
    taste
1 egg, beaten with 2 tablespoons heavy
    cream or milk

To make the pie crust, stir together the flour and salt in a bowl. Using 2 knives or your fingers, cut in the butter until the mixture forms coarse crumbs. Using a fork, stir in the water 1 tablespoon at a time, adding only enough for the pastry to hold together when pressed. Gather the dough into a ball and divide into 2 pieces, one slightly larger than the other. Wrap in plastic wrap and refrigerate.

To make the filling, pluck the grapes off their stems. You should have about 4 cups. Pinch them out of their skins, putting the insides into a saucepan and the skins into a bowl. Put the pan over medium heat, add ½ cup sugar, and cook until the grapes turn white, about 3 minutes. Pass them through a food mill placed over a bowl to rid them of their seeds, then add the skins to the pulp. Taste and, if it seems sour, add the remaining sugar while the pulp is still hot. Whisk in the flour or tapioca (use the larger amount of flour if the grapes were watery) and add the lemon zest and lemon juice. Let the mixture stand while you roll out the pie.

Preheat an oven to 450 degrees F. On a lightly floured board, roll the larger piece of dough into an 11-inch round. Ease it into a 9-inch pie pan and press it gently against the sides. Add the filling and brush the edges with water. Roll the second piece into a 9-inch round, set it over the filling, and crimp the edges. Make 2 slashes on the top for vents, and brush with the egg mixture.

Set the pie on a baking sheet in the center of the oven. After 10 minutes, lower the heat to 350 degrees F and bake until the crust is nicely browned, about 25 minutes. Remove to a rack to cool. Serve warm.

PERSIMMON PUDDING

SERVES 10

OWNERS OF PERSIMMON TREES MAY COMPLAIN OF THEIR DROPPINGS, BUT THEIR FRUITS DO MAKE A SUPERLATIVE WINTER PUDDING WITH A VARNISHED GOLDEN BROWN SURFACE. OUR NATIVE PERSIMMON IS A SMALL FRUIT—IT WOULD TAKE A DOZEN OR MORE FOR THIS PUDDING. BUT THE LARGE ACORN-SHAPED HACHIYA PERSIMMONS ARE IDEAL FOR THIS DESSERT. THEY SHOULD BE DEAD RIPE, THE CONSISTENCY OF JAM. IF YOU'RE PLANNING TO MAKE THIS FOR A SPECIFIC DAY, BUY YOUR PERSIMMONS A WEEK OR EVEN TWO AHEAD OF TIME TO ALLOW FOR RIPENING. PERSIMMON PULP CAN ALSO BE FROZEN UNTIL NEEDED. ❈ THIS PUDDING IS ESPECIALLY WONDERFUL WHEN SERVED WITH COLD CREAM POURED FROM A PITCHER, OR WITH SOFTLY WHIPPED AND SWEETENED CREAM.

4 soft, ripe Hachiya persimmons

1½ cups firmly packed light brown
    sugar

3 eggs, beaten

2 cups milk

1 teaspoon baking soda

½ cup butter, melted

1 teaspoon vanilla extract

1½ cups all-purpose flour

1 teaspoon baking powder

2 teaspoons ground cinnamon

1 teaspoon ground ginger

¼ teaspoon ground clove

¼ teaspoon salt

1 cup golden raisins (optional)

1 cup chipped pecans (optional)

Preheat an oven to 350 degrees F. Butter a 2½- to 3-quart baking dish or soufflé dish.

Using your hands, break up the persimmons then pass them through a food mill, skins and all. If you don't have a food mill, squeeze the pulp out of the skins, remove the seeds, and then purée the pulp in a blender. There should be 2 cups.

In a bowl, mix the pulp with the brown sugar, eggs, milk, baking soda, melted butter, and vanilla. In a second bowl, whisk together the flour, baking powder, spices, and salt. Gradually stir the flour mixture into the persimmon mixture to make a smooth batter, then add the raisins and nuts, if using.

Pour the batter into the prepared baking dish and bake until well browned and set, about 1 hour. The pudding should be firm to the touch but still a bit wobbly in the center. Transfer to a rack to cool slightly (the pudding will fall as it cools). Serve warm.

BAKED APPLE WITH CINNAMON CUSTARD SAUCE

SERVES 6

HOMEY AND UNPRETENTIOUS, A BAKED APPLE WITHOUT ITS SAUCE WAS ONCE COMMONLY SERVED AT THE BEGINNING OF THE DAY, RATHER THAN THE END. CHOOSE A NICE FAT APPLE, SUCH AS A ROME BEAUTY, GOLDEN DELICIOUS, OR CORTLAND. THE FILLING CAN VARY AS SUPPLY DICTATES—NUTS, RAISINS, AND SPICE FOR THE APPLE; SHERRY, SYRUP, OR CIDER IN THE PAN. AMOUNTS ARE APPROXIMATE, REFLECTING THE APPLES AT HAND AND THE SIZE OF THE CAVITIES.

Preheat an oven to 350 degrees F.

With an apple corer, remove the center of each apple, leaving the bottom intact. This space can be narrow or wide—in the case of the latter, it may need more filling. If you accidentally cut through the bottom, make a plug from the core and fit it into the hole. Peel the top third of each apple.

In a small bowl, mix together the butter, sugar, nuts, and a few raisins or other dried fruit. Fill the cavities with the mixture and set the apples in a baking dish so that they fit snugly together. Sprinkle with extra sugar and a dash of cinnamon.

Pour the liquid into the bottom of the dish to a depth of at least ¼ inch, and cover with aluminum foil. Bake until the apples are soft when pierced with the tip of a knife, from 30 minutes to an hour, depending on their size. Baste them 2 or 3 times while they're cooking.

To make the custard sauce, whisk together the egg yolks, sugar, and cinnamon in a saucepan. In a second pan, heat the milk until it almost reaches a boil. While it's heating, set a fine-mesh sieve over a bowl. Gradually whisk the hot milk into the egg yolks. Avoid making the mixture too frothy or it will be hard to "read" the spoon. Set the saucepan over low heat and cook, stirring constantly. Pull the spoon out frequently and glance at the back so that you can see if the custard is thickening. It should coat the spoon before it boils, and it shouldn't boil, so check frequently. As soon as it is done, pour it through the sieve. Stir in the vanilla. Let cool on the counter until tepid, stirring it occasionally to release the heat, then cover and refrigerate until cold.

Serve the apples warm with the cold custard sauce.

6 apples

6 tablespoons butter, at room temperature

6 tablespoons brown sugar or maple sugar, plus extra sugar for the top

½ cup finely chopped walnuts or pecans or toasted hazelnuts

raisins or dried currants, cranberries, or cherries

ground cinnamon

about 2 cups liquid such as maple syrup, apple cider, sherry, or water

Cinnamon custard sauce

2 large or 3 medium egg yolks

¼ cup sugar

1 tablespoon ground cinnamon

1½ cups milk

1 teaspoon vanilla extract

AMERICAN CHEESE PLATE

THERE ARE QUITE A FEW STELLAR AMERICAN CHEESES THAT CAN PROUDLY GRACE ANY TABLE—CHEESES MADE IN THE EUROPEAN STYLES, SUCH AS CHEDDAR, BRIE, MOZZARELLA, fresh and aged goat cheeses, and some fine American originals, such as Teleme and Monterey Jack. Wisconsin, the heart of America's dairyland, produces more than 250 specialty cheeses alone. Cheese making has been practiced for well over a century in the United States, but much cheese today is mass-produced and uniform, and does not bear the hand of the cheesemaker or the time needed for aging. For fine hand-crafted products, we need to look to smaller dairies that still make cheeses in the traditional ways. Whether they've been making cheese for generations or for just a few years, there are people who are passionately devoted to the craft and to maintaining one of our country's great culinary traditions.

A cheese plate can consist of a single cheese or several varieties. The most important thing to remember in any case is to serve the cheese at room temperature. There's little similarity between a piece of cold, hard cheese from the refrigerator and the same cheese left to stand at room temperature for a few hours. Neither the texture nor the flavor comes into its own until cheese warms up. Cheeses can be enjoyed with wine, sherry, ales, and pilsners, and served with breads or crackers. In general, you don't want a bread that will overwhelm the cheese, especially when serving a variety of them. But when enjoying a specific cheese alone, a certain bread like a dark rye or sourdough walnut may be ideal. Here are a few special American cheeses that can be found in good stores and through mail-order catalogs. Of course, there are many more dairies and cheeses than those mentioned—perhaps there are some even in your own area.

MONTEREY JACK: The genuine article is still made by the Vellas in Sonoma County, California, and by a few other small California cheese makers. Derived from cheeses made by the Spanish missionaries, a traditional Monterey Jack is nothing like the commercial lumpen white squares labeled Jack cheese. True Monterey Jack is delicate, but it has real flavor. There's a sharp little note at the end of each bite that sets off its otherwise pure, milky taste. The texture is creamy and smooth. Monterey Jack is great with a sourdough or mixed-grain breads, pears, and almonds.

DRY MONTEREY CHEESE: Wheels of Jack that have been aged from 6 to 14 months, dry Monterey Jack is a superb cheese—golden, rich, and nutty, not unlike a fine Parmesan. In fact, it can be used as a grating cheese or as an eating cheese. Its distinctive rind achieves its color by being rubbed with a mixture of cocoa and pepper.

MAYTAG BLUE: There are a number of hand-crafted blue cheeses, but Maytag blue is one of the best known. Made in Iowa and aged in caves, it has a nutty, rich flavor and creamy texture. It's a great choice for salads where blue cheese is complementary, or as a dessert cheese to accompany ripe pears, apples, and new crop walnuts.

RICE TELEME: This cheese with a Greek name is made by an Italian family in California's Central Valley. There are two kinds of Teleme, the commercial variety and the traditional Teleme, which is dusted with rice flour and aged longer than the commercial cheese. The latter is sold as rice Teleme, and this is the one to buy. Teleme is majestically creamy and soft, with a tart finish that shows off its delicacy. Once brought to room temperature, it practically flows out of its fragile skin.

It makes a marvelous grilled cheese sandwich and, spread on bread, a fine accompaniment to fruits and nuts.

GOAT CHEESES: The new American love for goat cheese may have started in California, but now many people are making goat cheeses all across the United States. Most shoppers know the fresh, creamy logs of goat cheese, but there are aged goats, pyramids, crottins, and even goat blues, goat Cheddars, and goat fetas. Capriole, in Kentucky, makes a fine aged goat cheese called My Old Kentucky Tome, which, in spite of the cute name, has a serious stature that makes it well worth seeking out.

CHEDDARS: Americans have long made cheddared cheeses, a holdover from our British heritage, and they're made all over the country. Upstate New York and Vermont are two prime producers of hand-crafted white Cheddars, some of the best-known being from Shelburne Farms and Cabot's Farmers' Co-op in Vermont. Some small Wisconsin dairies make excellent orange Cheddars. They are sold as young as day-old curds or aged 6 months and longer, until tangy and extra-sharp.

CROWLEY COLBY: At the Crowley's cheese factory in Vermont, this regional cheese is still made by hand. Colby is similar to a Cheddar, but it's softer and more moist, the texture not as tight. Real Colby cheese, such as this one, is a fine eating cheese with ample character.

WISCONSIN BRICK CHEESE: A washed rind cheese that ripens from the outside in, brick cheese—the name reflects not only its shape but the fact that bricks were once used to press out the moisture—is quite close in style to *Bier Käse*, or German beer cheese. Chalet Cheese in Monroe, Wisconsin, still produces a traditional hand-crafted brick that is smear ripened, meaning the bacteria, or smear, is wiped on the surface of the cheese. As it ages, the flavor becomes more earthy and rich. Brick is a cheese to enjoy with beer from one of our microbreweries, or a pilsner, and substantially flavored dark breads.

LIMBURGER: A Belgian surface-ripened cheese long made in Wisconsin, Limburger has an earthy, tangy flavor and pungent aroma. More of a lunch cheese than a dessert selection, Limburger is still an excellent choice for those who enjoy cheese with an assertive character. It is made by hand in Wisconsin and, like brick cheese, can be served with strongly flavored foods, such as dark rye, onions, and beer.

POPCORN

THE JAPANESE POP RICE FOR **GENMAI CHA,** AND THE MEXICANS POP AMARANTH FOR CARAMEL CANDY SQUARES, BUT I DON'T THINK ANOTHER NATION OBSESSES ABOUT POPCORN THE WAY AMERICANS DO. We used to eat it on a weekend night, with butter and salt. Now it's a snack to buy and eat anytime, anywhere.

All you need to make popcorn is a deep skillet with a lid—a big cast-iron one with a glass domed lid is perfect. Put about ⅓ cup corn kernels in the dry skillet over medium-high heat. Begin to slide the pan slowly back and forth over the fire, pausing now and then, so that the kernels move around and heat on all sides. Soon a few will start popping, then more and more, until eventually the pan is filled and just a few unpopped kernels remain.

Pour the popcorn into a big bowl, then toss with melted butter and sprinkle with salt. This is the old-fashioned kind. Today, health watchers might choose canola oil or unrefined corn oil in place of butter. You can also go beyond salt and add chile powder, black pepper, grated cheese, toasted spices, curry, or whatever moves your fancy.

INDEX

TABLE OF EQUIVALENTS

THE EXACT EQUIVALENTS IN THE FOLLOWING TABLES HAVE

BEEN ROUNDED FOR CONVENIENCE.

US/UK

oz=ounce
lb=pound
in=inch
ft=foot
tbl=tablespoon
fl oz=fluid ounce
qt=quart

METRIC

g=gram
kg=kilogram
mm=millimeter
cm=centimeter
ml=milliliter
l=liter

WEIGHTS

US/UK	Metric
1 oz	30 g
2 oz	60 g
3 oz	90 g
4 oz (¼ lb)	125 g
5 oz (⅓ lb)	155 g
6 oz	185 g
7 oz	220 g
8 oz (½ lb)	250 g
10 oz	315 g
12 oz (¾ lb)	375 g
14 oz	440 g
16 oz (1 lb)	500 g
1½ lb	750 g
2 lb	1 kg
3 lb	1.5 kg

OVEN TEMPERATURES

Fahrenheit	Celsius	Gas
250	120	½
275	140	1
300	150	2
325	160	3
350	180	4
375	190	5
400	200	6
425	220	7
450	230	8
475	240	9
500	260	10

LIQUIDS

US	Metric	UK
2 tbl	30 ml	1 fl oz
¼ cup	60 ml	2 fl oz
⅓ cup	80 ml	3 fl oz
½ cup	125 ml	4 fl oz
⅔ cup	160 ml	5 fl oz
¾ cup	180 ml	6 fl oz
1 cup	250 ml	8 fl oz
1½ cups	75 ml	12 fl oz
2 cups	500 ml	16 fl oz
4 cups/1 qt	1 l	32 fl oz

LENGTH MEASURES

⅛ in	3 mm
¼ in	6 mm
½ in	12 mm
1 in	2.5 cm
2 in	5 cm
3 in	7.5 cm
4 in	10 cm
5 in	13 cm
6 in	15 cm
7 in	18 cm
8 in	20 cm
9 in	23 cm
10 in	25 cm
11 in	28 cm
12 in/1 ft	30 cm

All-purpose (plain) flour/ dried bread crumbs/chopped nuts

¼ cup	1 oz	30 g
⅓ cup	1½ oz	45 g
½ cup	2 oz	60 g
¾ cup	3 oz	90 g
1 cup	4 oz	125 g
1½ cups	6 oz	185 g
2 cups	8 oz	250 g

Whole-Wheat (Wholemeal) Flour

3 tbl	1 oz	30 g
½ cup	2 oz	60 g
⅔ cup	3 oz	90 g
1 cup	4 oz	125 g
1¼ cups	5 oz	155 g
1⅔ cups	7 oz	210 g
1¾ cups	8 oz	250 g

Brown Sugar

¼ cup	1½ oz	45 g
½ cup	3 oz	90 g
¾ cup	4 oz	125 g
1 cup	5½ oz	170 g
1½ cups	8 oz	250 g
2 cups	10 oz	315 g

White Sugar

¼ cup	2 oz	60 g
⅓ cup	3 oz	90 g
½ cup	4 oz	125 g
¾ cup	6 oz	185 g
1 cup	8 oz	250 g
1½ cups	12 oz	375 g
2 cups	1 lb	500 g

Raisins/Currants/Semolina

¼ cup	1 oz	30 g
⅓ cup	2 oz	60 g
½ cup	3 oz	90 g
¾ cup	4 oz	125 g
1 cup	5 oz	155 g

Long-Grain Rice/Cornmeal

⅓ cup	2 oz	60 g
½ cup	2½ oz	75 g
¾ cup	4 oz	125 g
1 cup	5 oz	155 g
1½ cups	8 oz	250 g

Dried Beans

¼ cup	1½ oz	45 g
⅓ cup	2 oz	60 g
½ cup	3 oz	90 g
¾ cup	5 oz	155 g
1 cup	6 oz	185 g
1¼ cups	8 oz	250 g
1½ cups	12 oz	375 g

Rolled Oats

⅓ cup	1 oz	30 g
⅔ cup	2 oz	60 g
1 cup	3 oz	90 g
1½ cups	4 oz	125 g
2 cups	5 oz	155 g

Jam/Honey

2 tbl	2 oz	60 g
¼ cup	3 oz	90 g
½ cup	5 oz	155 g
¾ cup	8 oz	250 g
1 cup	11 oz	345 g

Grated Parmesan/Romano Cheese

¼ cup	1 oz	30 g
½ cup	2 oz	60 g
¾ cup	3 oz	90 g
1 cup	4 oz	125 g
1⅓ cups	5 oz	155 g
2 cups	7 oz	220 g